S0-BOJ-222

Living, Loving, and Laughing with Golden Retrievers

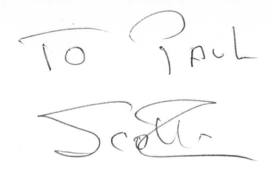

TO Paul

Scotty

Living, Loving, and Laughing with Golden Retrievers

Scotty Richardson

Copyright © 2015 by Scotty Richardson.

Library of Congress Control Number:		2015917170
ISBN:	Hardcover	978-1-5144-1784-3
	Softcover	978-1-5144-1783-6
	eBook	978-1-5144-1782-9

All rights reserved. No part of this book may be reproduced or transmitted in any form or by any means, electronic or mechanical, including photocopying, recording, or by any information storage and retrieval system, without permission in writing from the copyright owner.

Any people depicted in stock imagery provided by Thinkstock are models, and such images are being used for illustrative purposes only.
Certain stock imagery © Thinkstock.

Print information available on the last page.

Rev. date: 11/05/2015

To order additional copies of this book, contact:
Xlibris
1-888-795-4274
www.Xlibris.com
Orders@Xlibris.com
726442

SCOTTY'S TALES

PREAMBLE: LIVING, LOVING, AND LAUGHING WITH GOLDEN RETRIEVERS

When it began to appear that this book would become a reality, several folks suggested I needed to write a "foreword." Something about the author. Hmmmm. One of the most difficult things for me is to write about myself.

Nevertheless, I came up with the following: The author of these short stories is a seventy-three-year-old retired electrical supervisor. He's happily married, most of the time as much as any of you other married folks.

We have been proudly owned by a bevy of goldens and one wonderful Doberman in the last twenty-five years or so.

In chronological order, I think, here is the list:

Naomi, our wonderful Doberman

Peggy Sue, the first golden

Becky, second golden, a rescue

Earnie, a golden gift from a good friend

Burton, another gift, a happy boy

Porkchop, another gift from two great breeders in TX and NC, retired show dog

Harlow, Porkchop's daughter, also retired show dog and gift from a wonderful breeder in NC

Crunch, Harlow's son, a gift from NC at age three, current therapy and crisis response dog

Willy, our six-year-old "special" golden

Jasper, eight-month-old (young) little girl from Rome, PA, and a beauty! Hopefully, our next therapy dog!

The book covers the antics of the dogs through Burton, at which time I more or less gave up writing. So there is a lot of raw material out there yet!

For the last several years, we have been heavily into therapy work not only with our own dogs but also as evaluators for Pet Partners, a wonderful organization. It is such a pleasure to put a new team out there working in the community, bringing joy and relieving anxiety wherever they go!

So I figured the above should fulfill my obligation of telling the world about my life, right? Imagine my surprise when I was asked for more information. Now admittedly, these are the same people who insist I should set up a website. I continue to tell them that in order to have a website, you must first have an interesting life. Still they persisted. If you're easily bored, this might be a good place to stop reading. If not, well—your choice.

One thing you should know about my style of writing is that I find words similar to flatulence. Releasing a small burst offers minimal relief. Really letting fly offers much more relief. So I tend to be a bit wordy sometimes. Sorry about that. At least wordiness doesn't stink. Well, yeah, maybe sometimes it does. In order to gain any insight into the workings of my mind, I must digress. Or regress. Anyhow, we need to go back a few years. Prepare yourselves. This may be scary. I know it's not suitable for small children and/or budding criminals.

Memories of my childhood are limited. I was a sickly kid and had asthma from the get-go. My parents did the best they could raising my two brothers, my older sister, and myself. Unfortunately, they didn't possess much knowledge about raising children. This is probably because in the 1940s era, everyone just assumed they knew what they were doing when it came to raising kids (plus they were busy with a war and all). Same attitude most folks take when raising a puppy. Didn't need a lot of classes or education on the subject; you just knew how. Consequently, many families were pretty screwed up. Ours was one of them. Around age thirty-five during the latter stages of being treated for alcoholism, I learned the word "dysfunctional." But it is my belief that my parents did the best they could. They simply lacked knowledge and tools to really do the job right.

Plus I was a pretty rotten kid. It's a wonder they didn't just get rid of me. Maybe they tried. One of my earliest memories is being pushed down a long set of stairs in my Taylor-Tot stroller. To this day, I bear a big scar on my leg from that particular incident. I always wondered if that was an accident. Probably, but my older sister was reportedly in the area at the time (typical Richardson sense of humor). Possibly, I had tested my mom's patience beyond human endurance that day. I'll never be sure. I was also an inquisitive child, always testing my boundaries. I loved a good practical joke even at the tender age of seven or eight. I remember when my boyhood friend and I took the bus to downtown Portland, Oregon, where there was a marvelous joke and novelty shop. I bought a whole case of exploding cigarette loads. These were little items looking like a small toothpick. When inserted into a cigarette they exploded upon being lit. Wow! Great fun! Both my parents smoked! So I found a pack of my dad's cigarettes and loaded up a few of 'em! If my dad was curious why I was present every time he lit up the next day or so, he didn't show it. On the second day, he lit up. Settled into his chair and took a long drag. BOOM! That thing blew up so hard, it blew his wire-framed glasses clean off his face. Knowing full well I was in deep doo-doo, I headed out the door at warp speed. This didn't work. He was pissed, and he was fast. He caught me in the raspberry patch and beat the living crap out of me. I couldn't quit laughing all the time he wailed on me. Each time I looked into his blackened face, I'd laugh some more. Man, was I sore the next few days. That should have taught me a lesson. However, it didn't. I should mention here that my dad lost an eye during his teens due to some fireworks exploding in his face. Naturally, the fact that exploding items were expressly forbidden in our household only whetted my curiosity. But probably my lifetime-best exploding trick came about a year later. We lived on a small farm, maybe twenty-five acres or so. Most of this land was covered with blackberries and poison oak. Every spring we'd have this big land-clearing week. We'd take the tractor (which I was good at driving at the age of eight) and clear out massive piles of blackberry vines and brush. At the end of the clearing project came the bonfire! I always loved that bonfire— it was huge! Being a normal boy, I was something of a pyromaniac anyway. The week prior to our brush-grubbing project, one of the neighbor kids had brought me a real prize! He'd swiped an entire box of twelve-gauge shotgun shells from his dad. This kid and I spent quite a lot of time figuring out how best to use these shells. Finally, it was decided to take a short piece of two-inch conduit out of my dad's service truck. (My dad was an electrician too.) This pipe was threaded on both ends, perhaps one-foot long. We screwed a pipe cap on one end of it and proceeded to empty each and every shotgun shell—powder, shot, and all—into this budding pipe bomb. Once we unloaded all the shells into it, we screwed a cap on the other end of it. Knowing what I know today about gunpowder, why we weren't killed is still a mystery. The plan was to toss this thing into the bonfire the next week. I remember how the anticipation was killing us!

The big day came. We'd piled brush and blackberry vines as high as the house! The bonfire was placed about 150 feet behind the house. Just before dinner, as was the custom, my dad lit the fire using some old tires and gasoline to get it going. Once it was going pretty well, everybody went into the house for dinner. I was the last one in because I'd taken the prized pipe bomb from its hiding place under the house and tossed it into the fire. I then casually sauntered into the house, taking my spot at the table with the family. Waiting, waiting—seemed like eternity—trying to act normal. Then halfway through the meal came an explosion I haven't experienced the likes of to this day! My dad, sitting across the table from me, had a full load of mashed potatoes on his fork headed for his mouth. He missed his mouth and spilled spuds all down the front of him. There he sat, fork still poised, stunned look on his face. After what seemed forever, he jumped up and ran to the back of the house. Wow! My pipe bomb had exceeded all our expectations! All the windows in the back of the house were blown out. The bonfire had been blown to bits—there were small fires for several hundred feet in every direction. It resembled a scene from *Dante's Inferno*. As I watched my dad running around stomping out fires, I knew my only hope for survival was to lie and lie well. But luck was with me; my dad didn't even consider that I was capable of a disaster of this magnitude. He thought he'd left the gas can too close to the fire. Good theory, as the explosion vaporized the gas can too! He never found out until he lay on his deathbed with lung cancer at age seventy-four. I finally told him. He said, "I knew you must have had something to do with that! I just knew it!"

As I mentioned earlier, I was a sickly, scrawny kid. I wore glasses at the age of seven. This, of course was a continual source of amusement to the bigger kids who needed someone to pick on. I got real tired of being picked on. But physically, I just wasn't big enough to duke it out. So I got devious. One kid in particular constantly picked on me. He happened to be our paper boy. He was three years older and seventy-five pounds heavier. This was a fat nasty kid, even by today's standards. Our house was situated on a steep hill. The hill was about half-mile long, with our house near the middle. Every day this kid would ride his paper-laden bike up the hill, always being sure to stop to toss a few rocks at me or call me "four-eyes" if I was around. On his return trip down the hill, he'd really be moving, his stops all done. One day, I'd had enough. Armed with my mom's broom, I lay in wait in the ditch alongside the road. I made sure I was near the bottom of the hill where this mean kid would reach maximum velocity. Down the hill he came, probably doing thirty miles per hour or so on his bike. Timing was everything here. At the exact split second, I popped out of the ditch and jammed that broomstick through his front wheel. I didn't even need to run! The fat kid left about half his face in the gravel during his long slide on his belly and head; destroyed the bike too. Problem was, I hadn't thought past this point in my retaliation. The kid's parents came and scraped him off the pavement then called my folks. Yup! My old man beat the crap out of me again! My dad was mad because he had to buy that kid a new bike. Later when the whole story came out, my dad apologized to me for the whipping. That was the last time the fat kid picked on me though—so it was worth it!

Around this point in my life, age eight or so, I developed my work ethic. My dad did the best he could, but work was short in those days, and we were poor. There were times we didn't have enough to eat. If my sister or I wanted any school clothes, we had to work for them. I started picking strawberries, beans, and hops during the summers. The bus would pick us up at 5:00 a.m. and off we'd go to the fields for the day. Back then, the field bosses were almost always one of our schoolteachers out to make a few extra bucks for the summer. These field bosses were strict! No berry-throwing (I was a good shot!); you had to pick your rows clean. I got fired a lot, usually for throwing berries. One time, I was canned for locking the field boss in the outhouse. Nobody would let her out. Hot that day too. She also happened to be my sixth grade teacher. She hollered at the top of her lungs for a couple of hours before one of the farm owners discovered her plight. She wasn't too happy when they let her out. They fired several of us that day. But my folks would always call her and swear I'd be a good kid, please take me back, we needed the money, and so forth. I always got rehired. I was a fast picker, and there weren't enough pickers most of the time anyway. I picked berries and beans all the way through high school. If you wanted new clothes, that's the way you got them.

Dogs: That's what this is eventually leading into. My folks got our first dog when I was perhaps nine years old. Our dogs were always "outside" dogs—no dogs in the house. I guess I learned to love animals early on, probably from my dad, who loved all animals, and my grandmother who was living with us at the time. My grandmother brought an old dog named "Bootsie" with her when she moved in with us. Bootsie was a Heinz 57 variety, as I look back, probably mostly yellow Labrador. Bootsie was a lover. Even though the rule was "no dogs in the house," I always managed to sneak in the ol' girl (Bootsie, not my grandmother) when the weather was bad. She was pretty crippled up with arthritis, and the cold weather really bothered her (both Bootsie and my grandmother). My dad would allow it if he were home. I loved that old dog, and so did my grandmother. I guess we had Bootsie for six or seven years. One evening, she went missing. I looked long into the night. The next morning, I found her dead under a tree in the woods. She had dug a big hole, laid herself down in it—and died. This is my first memory of death. I missed that dog desperately.

This began a series of family dogs. I remember "Daisy May," an Airedale. She was a great dog! She's smart and a lot of fun. We lost Daisy May to a big earth-grader during freeway construction above our home. Then there was "Koo-nah," an Indian word for "friend." Koo-nah was pure collie and dumb as a box of rocks. We also had a huge blonde cat at the time that purely hated Koo-nah. This cat would lie on a low-hanging branch of the big maple tree in the back yard. In order to get to the water dish, Koo-nah always took the same route, right under that limb. The cat would leap on Koo-nah's back and hold on while riding this howling, terrified dog 100 feet or so before dropping off and sauntering back to the porch with a satisfied look on his face. This scene was repeated several times a day. Koo-nah never learned to look up or to change his route. This became our afternoon entertainment. Koo-nah eventually developed a terrible skin condition and had to be put down. I probably learned my love of storytelling in my early teen years— strangely from a hobo who went by the name of "Old Johnny." Below our house was an RR track. If we walked that track for about a mile, we came to a switchyard. This was not a busy switchyard, just a place where the RR left a few cars now and then. Every summer, a number of hobos would set up a camp there. Because a few of my friends and I played there often, we became friends with some of these homeless men. One of the regulars was a man known only as Old Johnny. Old Johnny probably hadn't seen fifty yet, but to us he seemed to be an old man. Certainly, he'd had a hard life. And this man was a storyteller. We would sit, enthralled, next to his cardboard shelter and his cook fire while he regaled us with his stories of the road. Sometimes on dark afternoons, he'd tell us ghost stories! He was fascinating. All the more so, naturally, because our parents had expressly forbidden us to go anywhere near these hobos. But the lure of another of Old Johnny's fabulous stories was always too much for us. We'd sneak away and spend a lazy summer afternoon listening to this gentle soul weave his yarns for our entertainment. One day, we went back after having been away a few days from the "Hobo Jungle" (as our parents called it) to find the entire area burned to the ground. The huts—gone. All the men gone too. We never saw Old Johnny again, but I can still see his sad dark eyes and remember some of his stories when I close my eyes and dream of days gone by. How that old man could make us laugh! He had a gift. I dreamed that someday I could tell a story the way he could. I doubt I ever will.

So now you know something of my childhood. I could go on and on; lots more stories to tell. I could tell you of how we derailed a train. No one was hurt, but that was my first brush with the long arm of the law! I could tell you of our "forts" and the initiation rites of young boys to these exclusive clubs. I could tell of the tree houses, of falling into the manure pile at the end of the barn, and of being stuck in blackberries while up to my armpits in cow shit (my parents had to cut a path to get me out), or about burning the poison oak and getting poison oak in my larynx, and the trip to the hospital. But let's skip ahead a few years. Let's get to the point where I'm married to the love of my life, where we buy a home and acquire the first dog of our marriage!

The year is 1965. We are up to our armpits again, this time in debt. We purchase a house, a new car, and a new pickup truck—all at the same time. (These were learning years.) Michael is about to become pregnant with our daughter. I am still very much into hunting and fishing—bird hunting is my current passion. I talk my wife into allowing me to buy a birddog and name her "Ingrid." She's a gorgeous German short-haired pointer. I build her a big dog-pen on the back of the garage, complete with a cute little doghouse. Being young and probably even dumber than I am today, I figure I could have this dog field-trained and ready for hunting season that fall. *Ha!* Between having to work a lot to make ends meet and having some life outside of work, training time was scarce. Worse, I had no earthly idea of how to train a dog. I thought I knew; dog training was simple, right? None of the dogs we had during my childhood had ever had any training; they were outside dogs treated like property not like family. I tried and tried to get this dog trained, but I only had a few minutes each day to spend with her. She proved to be a good hunter, all right—she just didn't want to hunt for me. She wanted to hunt for herself. Once we got to the fields, Ingrid would take off and chase every bird into the next county. I never got close enough to a pheasant to even get a good look at it, much less shoot it. Worse, the neighbors were complaining bitterly about Ingrid's excessive barking. It seems that when we were gone all day working, she would vocalize. She stopped when we got home. I was too stupid to know she was lonely. Finally, we gave her away to a family who owned a big farm out in the country. Within a year, Ingrid turned into a marvelous companion for this family and their children. They had the time to spend with this energetic, very driven dog. Ingrid even rode in the Grand Marshall's car during their Harvest Day's Parade—a happy ending for the dog.

Speaking of parades, one of the biggest parades in the country is held during the Portland, Oregon, Annual Rose Festival. The Port of Portland donated the use of some of their huge warehouses to the float builders, most of whom travel from town to town designing and building these huge flower-bedecked apparitions for one day's use. One of these contractors came to Portland every year and brought his Doberman pinscher "Terra" with him. Now having watched a lot of TV and movies, I was pretty sure that all Dobermans were savage, vicious creatures. You know, rip your heart out of your chest; eat it while it's still beating. Imagine my surprise upon finding Terra to be a playful, friendly creature who wanted nothing more than having her head rubbed. I fell in love with this beautiful animal. Her owner quickly caught on that Terra and I had a thing going. He wanted to take a fishing trip but couldn't take Terra. Would I take her home for a few days? I leapt at the chance! Michael was less anxious than I was, not having been around Terra and knowing she was a Doberman! But Michael—always the patient soul—said yes. So Terra came home with me for a few days. Fate? Maybe. Michael also fell hard for this lithe, beautiful creature.

And so it was that after Terra was reunited with her owner, we knew we wanted a Doberman. But being uneducated on the finer points of dog breeding, we found Naomi through a backyard breeder. We didn't know that puppies should be seven weeks old before bringing them home. "Naomi," as our daughter named her, was only four weeks old when she came home with us. Her back legs wouldn't work right; she was still so young and wobbly. But it was love from the first! She grew quickly and was smart as a whip. About the time Naomi was a year old, I had begun running daily. Like most reformed drinkers or smokers, I felt the need to do something healthy for a change. Running with Naomi became as natural as could be! When she saw me lacing up my Nikes, she'd begin dancing and whirling in anticipation! Thus it was, she ran daily with me for many years—a true bonding experience. Naomi also accompanied our daughter to her soccer games, becoming a sideline icon so to speak—the team mascot!

Naomi was close to all of our family. She was protective but never overly so. I remember a time our foster daughter Tami and our daughter Barbra were playing in the front yard, and the play got a bit rough. Naomi leaped between the girls and me with a "that's enough!" look on her face, paws on my chest. I wasn't even involved! She seemed to sense when play got carried away. My younger brother decided he could wrestle Naomi into submission one day in the front yard. "Heck, she's only a sixty-pound dog," he said. He tried to pin her down. Once she realized what he was up to, there was a furious whirling of bodies—hers and my brother's. This wrestling match ended abruptly with my brother flat on his back, and Naomi sitting on his chest with fangs bared. After I rescued my brother, he never tried that trick again!

These were good years. I worked a lot: an eighty-hour week was not unusual. Overtime in those years was paid at double-time. With this extra money, we placed our daughter in a good private school and began saving for college, and hopefully, an early retirement. Finally, the day came. Our daughter was off to Pomona College, outside of Los Angeles,

California. It was a sad day for us—a sadder day for Naomi. The poor dog was devastated. But dogs tend to be adaptable (more than humans anyway), and I was still running seven to ten miles a day with Naomi. She became "my dog" during those years. It just happened. Probably, it was because of the bonding from all the running, hiking, and evening mountain bike rides that she joined me on. I loved that dog. We all did. Naomi was still running daily with me and doing three thirty-five mile bike loops a week in addition to the running at age eleven. It was on one of these bike rides that she was attacked by a bunch of hornets. This attack apparently triggered a series of strokes, leaving her with no control of her bowels. She went from an active, athletic animal to being very limited, practically overnight. Our vet said there was little we could do. We literally lived our lives around her bodily functions until she was thirteen years old when her condition worsened. Finally, the dreaded decision was made. Naomi would be put out of her misery. For those of you who have lived through this heart-wrenching decision, you know the pain, the guilt, the indecision, and the grief that follows. On the appointed morning, we took Naomi up to one of her favorite trails, allowing her to walk one more time in an area where she had run hundreds of times. She wobbled along with us, her hindquarters not working very well. Somehow, I believe she knew this was the day. Perhaps, she sensed our grief. Certainly, it was palpable. We then took her over to the river where she swam a little for the last time. But the time came. We took her to the vet's office where she literally died in our arms. Oh how we cried. As I write this, tears are once again in my eyes. I loved that dog as much as anything on the face of this earth. I would have happily cut off an arm to have her just one more year. Michael felt the same way. But you can't do that. You must let go. That doesn't mean it's easy though. It's not. Here we are forty years later and I still feel the grief. I always will. Nothing can replace the unconditional love you receive from a pet. I know Naomi and I will run together again at the Rainbow Bridge, along with the goldens we have lost. I know this. For a year, we could not bring ourselves to get another dog. No other dog could ever replace Naomi. Certainly, I would never be able to bring another Doberman into my life. No other Doberman could ever measure up to Naomi, and it wouldn't be fair to compare the new dog to the old. But as time blunted our grief, we started thinking. Perhaps we should look for another dog. But what kind? Not a Doberman, that we knew. We asked a friend of ours who works as a veterinary technician what sort of dog should we get. She suggested a golden retriever. A golden retriever? We didn't think so. After many years of living with a Doberman and the macho image she projected, perhaps my male ego couldn't quite cope with having a dog I might need to protect, instead of the other way around. Goldens just didn't fit the image I was seeking. They seemed a little "wimpy" to me. Besides, Michael had made a decision to find a smaller dog this time around—something in the thirty-five-pound range to cut down on the dirt and dog hair in the house. Wow, was God ever about to play a joke on us! We just didn't sense it yet. So we looked at many breeds. Staffordshire Terriers? Too stubborn. Maybe a Collie or an Irish Setter? No, too dumb. Also too big and hairy! (Ha!) During our search, we happened to attend a Fall Foray hosted by the Oregon Mycological Society, a group dedicated to studying mushrooms of which we had been members for many years. Fate intervened once again. The foray was held at a church camp, and the camp dog was—a golden retriever!

This dog and I hit it off immediately! Her name was "Sunny." Sunny would show up wherever Michael and I were hunting mushrooms, far back in the woods. She'd come past our camper to get her head rubbed. She liked me. And it was mutual. Her owners were a bit concerned she would go home with us. Sunny didn't come home with us, but she sent the knowledge home that we needed a golden retriever, just like Sunny. The search was on! We went back to our friend, the vet tech, armed with this new conviction. She was ecstatic because she'd been trying to tell us for months that a golden was right for us. She even knew of just the right goldens! In her fourteen years of experience at the clinic, there were some goldens that just stood out head and shoulders above the average. Smart, good hips, great disposition—they had it all according to her. She placed a call to these breeders, asking when they planned another litter of pups. Alas, they had made the decision that the male was too old; there would not be another batch of puppies from these two dogs. We were disappointed but still firm in our decision to find just the right golden.

We began shopping the ads. Once again, we knew no way to find a dog other than in the newspapers. We looked at quite a few pups but ruled them all out for one reason or another. Too wild. Too expensive. Until we found "Peggy Sue!" Peggy Sue came out of a good breeder.

We were just lucky—the woman had placed an ad for this batch of pups in our local paper. Usually, her dogs were gone, word of mouth. Peggy Sue's dad, "Buster," met us at the door with his dinner dish in his mouth. What a friendly dog! Darn, the pups were only two weeks old; we'd have to wait over a month to bring her home. So the money was put down, the contract signed, and we had purchased our first golden retriever. Pretty heady stuff!

The very next week, we got a call from the vet tech. Fate's fickle finger was at work again. One of the pups, now over a year old, had come back to the breeder she had told us about. Were we interested in taking this dog? "Oh, shoot," we told her, "we just bought a dog!" Well, could we at least take this dog for a couple of weeks until they found a new owner? It seems the breeder's other dogs were not happy about this dog being returned, and they feared for the life of this dog if they kept her much longer. Had to close her in a bedroom where their dogs couldn't get to her. "Sure we said, what the heck?" We had close friends who were vacationing in Mexico at the time, and we knew they were looking for a dog. They had lost their Irish Setter just the year before. So it appeared this might work out for everybody. Over to the breeder's house, we went. When this dog was dragged, terrified, out of the back bedroom, it almost broke our hearts. Dirty, skinny, matted hair, covered with fleas—a pathetic creature. We managed to get her into our van as gently as possible, where she proceeded to soil herself in fear. Each time we passed under a bridge or a road sign, she'd duck and cower in terror. After arriving home, we bathed her, groomed her and tried to help her over her fear. In less than forty-eight hours, I fell completely, hopelessly, in love with this marvelous creature. It was mutual. We soon realized we were destined to be a two-dog family. After our friends returned from Mexico, they took one look at this dog and I together. The bond we'd formed was obvious. They said, "We think she's your dog."

So she was! If you can stomach reading the rest of this book after this lengthy foreword, you'll know this dog is none other than "Becky," my first heart dog. I wrote a post dedicated to this wonderful companion the summer of 1998 just before the Golden Retriever National Specialty in Seattle, where we entered Becky in the Parade of Rescues. My post tells you all you need to know about what I feel for this dog.

We'd only had Becky a few weeks when our puppy Peggy Sue was brought home to stay. Becky wasn't too happy to share her newfound happiness with another dog. But after a few weeks of being a bit standoffish, Becky accepted this new dog into her life. She realized nobody was leaving. Peggy Sue too is a sweetheart; her disposition borders on angelic. However, my posts will tell you more about Peggy Sue than you may ever want to know. For the record, we loved her and all her little quirks. We wouldn't have traded her for anything. This brings us into that current time frame, where the posts I wrote to the G&H list will tell you all the details—or tales, if you will—about these dogs we lived with and loved so much. You'll find out about the third dog, "My Son Earnie," and how he came to be. How we loved this golden boy! He could make us laugh even on our darkest days. Then came a series of other wonderful dogs, doing therapy work and improving ours and others lives.

Just one more thing I need to tell you is how we found the G&H list on the Internet. It was fate, once more. Having recently gotten "online" with my computer, I stumbled across the late Helen Redlus's "Golden Retrievers in Cyberspace" website after having looked up "golden retrievers" with one of the search engines. From there, I found the Golden@Hobbes list—a listserv dedicated solely to golden retrievers and their humans. This was in April of 1995. It rapidly became apparent what a truly "golden" resource this list is! The advice from many true experts is simply amazing. The people on the list were, and to this day are, some of the nicest people ever to grace the planet. The education regarding raising pups, etc. we've gotten from the experts on this list has been invaluable. If you read some of my early posts regarding how we trained Peggy Sue, you'll see how ignorant we really were. If you read on, you'll see how much we've learned in a little over thirty-five years. Plus, the education is continual; we're still learning, much to the benefit of our canine companions. Thank doG Earnie didn't have to suffer what we put poor Peggy Sue through with our utter stupidity.

At any rate, I have found my niche. I've always enjoyed writing humor—and certainly I wanted and needed someone to share the antics of these golden goofballs with. The G&H list became that forum. Many mornings, I awaken with a story in my cranium, rattling around in there like a marble in a fishbowl. The G&H list has given me an outlet for these stories, a place to share them, and a place to hopefully amuse others with our dogs' hilarious antics! Over time, I have found that many people seem to enjoy the humor in my posts. Others, of course,

I just annoy. Can't please everybody, right? But the vast majority seems to want more of these stories, and I was, and am, happy to share them. I never cease to marvel at the knowledge, kindness, and generosity of folks on the G&H list. If you look at this through my eyes, it's pretty amazing. A list of over two thousand people, most of whom own one or more golden retrievers, which is the common bond. A man who has freely given of his time, his knowledge, and his money continues to run the list. I have never met Wade Blomgren, the G&H list administrator, face to face. He lurks in the background, sort of the benevolent List God. He rarely intervenes unless someone gets too abusive or foul language is used. Wade does his job well. If things get out of hand, he takes care of it. In his own words, "this is not a democracy!" Fortunately, rarely does Wade need to intervene—such is the tone of the G&H list. Sure like any extended family, which this list resembles, there are disagreements. Topics that can never be agreed upon, any more than the Jews will ever completely agree with the Palestinians. That doesn't mean somebody's right or wrong; it just proves there are different opinions in any large, diverse group.

Any doubt I might have had about the kindness and caring of the G&H "listers" as I call them, was certainly removed in November of 1996. At the tender age of fifty-four, with less than six months to go before my planned early retirement, I was diagnosed with prostate cancer. That has to be proof that God has a wicked sense of humor. Being told you have cancer is a difficult thing to digest. First you're scared. Then you're depressed. Then at least in my case, you're pissed off. Talk about unfair! All the years we went without stuff so I could retire early! If I had croaked before getting to spend some of my retirement funds, it would really have cheesed me off. But during the surgery and my recovery, I learned firsthand of the kindness and caring of the G&H listers: I received well over one hundred e-mails, cards, etc. from folks I'd never laid eyes on! Believe me, during really rough times, little things like that mean a lot. There were days I was so miserable that death didn't look so bad. The kindness and caring shown me by list members carried me through a lot of nasty days.

Since that time, other members of the G&H list have been the beneficiaries of the golden kindness of so many marvelous individuals. Some have been ill, also with cancer; some have had other crises. In each case the G&H "listers" have come through either with their time, cards, or money to help those in need. If you try putting that in perspective, you can't. It's just too incredibly unthinkable. Many listers have put in a lot of their personal time and money to help raise funds necessary to save goldens left in animal shelters, in need of medical care and/or owners. During my time on the G&H list, there have been many forms of fundraisers. All have one thing in common: helping the dogs! We all feel the need to help dogs left by uncaring individuals, discarded as if they were pieces of trash in many cases. Other times perhaps, a family must give up a beloved pet for some reason. These are the dogs we try to help. God knows these loving animals deserve a far better fate than being deserted in animal shelters, left to die.

So we come to the purpose of this book. My dream is that people will buy a copy of this book to help generate funds for Golden Rescue. I want nothing out of this project other than the pride that comes with the knowledge that somewhere, I had a hand in helping out an animal that otherwise may have been euthanized. If this book saves just one dog, I'm happy. And if some of you find the content of it amusing, I'm happy. Right now—speaking of happy—I have three golden retrievers at my feet imploring me to get off this #&!% computer and play with them. So be it!

Scotty Richardson
February 2015

THE GREAT CUCUMBER RACE

Following the "natural foods" thread—you ain't lived until you've witnessed a "cucumber race!" These races are held only during the growing season which is somewhat short here in SW Washington.

We garden a small plot on our neighbor acreages where we raise numerous veggies. Becky loves veggies, particularly cucumbers. Given a choice between steak and cucumbers—cucumbers win, seeds down. Peggy Sue couldn't care less about veggies. But she will sneak into the garden and snitch a large cucumber just to tantalize Becky with it. She walks up to Becky with this humungous cuke in her jaws and a look on her face that says "nyah nyah! I've got a cuke and YOU DON'T!" At this point, the race is on. My neighbor has a huge lawn, over an acre, and around and around they go.

Becky is faster, but Peggy Sue turns sharper. Eventually, Becky will get a hold of the cuke, and they will tug and rip it to shreds. Becky will then proceed to devour the remains. At this point, Peggy Sue goes back to the garden for more ammunition—and the race begins again!

I have often thought my neighbor must wonder why there are cucumbers all over his lawn. Sort of a variation on the 400-yard relay race?

Becky (Gimmeee that cuke, you impudent puke!)
Peggy Sue (Catch me if you can; veggie biter!)

Michael and Scotty Richardson
Becky and Peggy Sue (The Golden Girls—Arf! Arf!)

CHARMIN', JUST CHARMIN'

A fine, crisp fall morning here in the Northwest. A perfect day for a mushroom hunt! Off to the woods with the dogs and my wife! It's a perfect morning, the mushrooms plentiful. Michael is off up the hill, I am down in a canyon. The dogs are off doing dog things. All is well. We regroup on the trail. Michael wrinkles her nose and glares at me accusingly. "Did you?"

"No," says I, "I thought it was you—!"

At this point, all eyes focus on Becky who is sitting on the trail with the original s***-eating grin on her face. "Oh no!" exclaims the master. Dog looks *very* guilty. This is the dog I shared my sandwich with. She drinks out of my water bottle. I have been throwing a stick for her. I smell my hand. There is no doubt. So much for the fresh autumn air. We head for the truck to get the Tic Tacs we stupidly left behind. Dog eats Tic Tacs. Now smells about like someone took a dump under a pine tree, but this is an improvement.

Does anyone have a cure for this disgusting situation? No, not a cure for the dog. That's probably impossible. A cure for the inconsiderate lazy jerk that caused the problem because they don't know how to s*** in the woods!

I will share a fantasy with you if I may (fantasies change when you're over fifty). I picture myself in camouflage clothing, Becky with a camouflage doggy-pack. Her pack contains a supply of cheap plastic trowels and some manuals complete with graphics providing explicit instructions on how to s*** in the woods. For reasons obvious to the reader, Becky will be wearing a muzzle.

We hide on the trailhead. We follow a group of hikers. As one individual with a strained look on his face laterals into the woods, we covertly follow him. Just as he drops his trousers, we leap out of the brush shouting, "Freeze! It's Mr. Poopers and his wonder dog, Becky!" I will have a shotgun. "Capitulate or die, scum bucket," I will shout. He will read the manual. Becky will pass him a trowel. He will do his business properly forever after.

Becky and I will be famous. We will do product endorsements for Kohler and Charmin'. We will be on Oprah, and Geraldo will call us. We will be internationally known and feared.

Fifty years from now, when children go to the woods, their parents won't say "look out for the bears." They will say "beware of Mr. Poopers and Becky." No one will drop their trousers in the outdoors without first looking furtively around them and digging a proper hole in which to do their business.

Becky (Geez, Dad, I know it stinks but it tastes better than those Tic Tacs.)
Peggy Sue (Why is Becky riding home in the back of the bus?)

Michael & Scotty Richardson
Becky & Peggy Sue (The Golden Girls—Arf! Arf!)

TRICKS TO PLAY ON
YOUR MASTERS

Hello! My name is Peggy Sue; the astute readers will recognize me as the sophisticated half of "The Golden Girls." Becky and I own Scotty and Michael Richardson. I have learned a couple of things that drive my dad nuts! One is my continued pursuit of the fine art of scatology. I have studied this for about four years now and expect to earn my PU degree soon. Dad gets really anal about this habit.

One other cute trick is my affinity for VW seat belts. I'm sure all of you have heard of Fahrvergnügen? Well, how about "arfvergnügen? The former, loosely translated, means "joy of driving." The latter, "arfvergnügen" means the joy of eating VW seat belts! I discovered the wonderful consistency of the plastic buckles first and the joy of listening to them snap and crackle as I cheerfully masticated away. Then I moved on to the belts themselves, and discovered that it's possible to completely sever them with a bit of effort. This really sends the old man into orbit because when somebody gets into the van and tries to put on their belt, all they find are two halves with mangled buckles! :-)

It all works for Becky and I though, because after a seat belt session, Dad would load us into the van, and we took long trips out to the VW graveyard for another six-pack of seat belts. We got to bark at the cows and stuff.

And hey, Mom put some hot sauce on the last set of seat belts. This really spruced up the flavor, they were tasteless before. I love Mexican! I wonder what she'll put on them next?

Becky (I don't know what you see in those seat belts, this bone tastes better.)
Peggy Sue (You wouldn't know, field-bred bitch. It's an acquired taste, like caviar.)

Michael & Scotty Richardson
Becky & Peggy Sue (The Golden Girls—Arf! Arf!)

MOUSE TRAPS PREVENT COUNTERSURFING!

Ah yes, mouse traps! It's probably OK to use them, but we put them upside down under a sheet of newspaper. This not only reduces the possibility of harming your canine friends, but it makes a great racket when they are sprung. We used this method on our late cat, Isabel, as well as on the dogs if they tried to get on the furniture.

A friend of mine tried everything with his beagle to keep him off his easy chair and, in desperation, wired a fence charger to the chair. There is a God. He forgot about the fence charger and sat in the chair. He said it worked, but he removed the fence charger, turned the chair over to his beagle, and sat on the couch.

Becky (Aw Dad, you know I only get to sit on the recliner with you! I never get on the furniture! I'm *such* a good dog! How about a cookie?) Pigger Sue (I sleep on the futon with Mom. All my feet are in the air, and I look sooooo cozy! Who could stand to chase me off? Cookie? What cookie?)

Michael & Scotty Richardson
Becky & Peggy Sue (The Golden Girls—Arf! Arf!)

COLD WATER—HAH!

How cold is too cold? We certainly haven't discovered the low cut-off temperature with our girls. On a winter outing to Ramona Falls, a pristine area on the slopes of Mt.

Hood about seventy-five miles from here in Oregon, we took a *brisk* hike with our two clowns. The temperature was around 10° F and the wind from the east at about 30 mph. Cold. Very cold for this area.

There is a fair-sized branch of the Salmon River that runs through the area, runs very swiftly, or it would freeze solid. All the rocks around the stream were covered with inches of ice. Treacherous! But guess who decided (on their own!) that a good swim was on the menu? Well, it wasn't my wife or I!

Both dogs were covered with so much ice frozen in their fur that they "tinkled" like little bells as the ice cycles hanging from their feathers swung about like wind chimes! There was no sign of discomfort at all. The biggest problem was on the way home in the Hairmobile when they thawed out! It took several days to dry out the car!

I doubt we'll ever know what temperatures are too low for these dogs unless we move to the North Pole!

Becky (Yeah! That was "really cool." We slid around on the rocks and ate icicles like they were ready made doggy treats!)

Peggy Sue (I bet I weighed one hundred pounds! And hey, Dad, why are you shivering?

This is great!)

Michael & Scotty Richardson
Becky & Peggy Sue (The Golden Girls—Arf! Arf!)

HUNTIN' DAWG!

Following the thread on how our dogs hunt, thought I'd jump in! Becky has a *powerful* hunting instinct, unlike Peggy Sue who will (I have seen this!) sit within three feet of a squirrel looking it in the eyes. I think they communicate. Peggy Sue has no desire to *kill* anything.

But Becky—that's another matter! I have been able to call her off of cats, deer, etc., when she decided to chase, but I discovered there is a critter she simply cannot control herself over—squirrels!

We have an *overabundance* of Douglas squirrels in our yard. Every year this time, they come to try and rob the bird feeders. The feeders are squirrel-resistant, but they hang on the feeders and scare off the birds. Not being a killer type anymore, I have trapped them for the last two years and relocated them; usually across a river or freeway and away from the bus lines. As clever as they are about robbing my feeders, I'm sure they are capable of purchasing a bus ticket and coming home.

Becky lies near the patio door and watches the trap. If I get a squirrel, she moans loudly and emits a high, keening noise, pressing her nose so hard against the glass that her nose bends at a ninety-degree angle. Talk about dog snot on the glass! I made the mistake of letting her out into the yard with a squirrel in the trap. I had *no control* over her—she charged the trap with gusto, flipping it high in the air, trying to rattle the poor critter out of it.

Also on one of our *freedom rides* to free a squirrel (I put sixty miles on the van this weekend driving squirrels to a new home), I took the girls along in the Hairvagen to a local park. I lifted the tailgate to the van and lowered but didn't latch it. When I released the squirrel, Becky blasted the back door of the Hairmobile open, and the chase was on!

Poor squirrel felt dog breath on that one, I'll tell you! So far this year, we have relocated ten squirrels and still they hang off the feeders!
Oh well, as long as the trap is in the yard, I won't have to look far for Becky!

Becky (Lemmee have one, pleeeeaaase? I won't hurt him much, just wanna munch him a little!)
Peggy Sue (Hey what's the big deal? I'd rather have a cookie!)

Michael & Scotty Richardson

HAIRBALL?

All this talk about the uses of dog hair got me to thinking, and sometimes, that's dangerous. Ask my wife.

It got me to thinking about the fact that I am envious of all the wonderful hair my dogs so willingly share with me. It's on my clothes. In my shoes. On the carpets. The drapes. The salad. It rolls out from under the seats in the Hairvagen van in melon-sized balls. It's everywhere except where I would like it to be. On my head!

Being over fifty and rapidly becoming "follically impaired," I envy these exceedingly hairy beasts. I still remember the 1960s when we were refused restaurant service in California because of beards and long hair. (I'm proud of that!)

Now the most hair I see in a day is in the washbowl.

Thought I would like to see what I looked like as a redhead—so I had Becky sit on my head. This was OK except for her occasional anal gland problem. Won't repeat that one. If you try this at home, be sure your dog is facing the same way you are. Smells better. And you can look in the mirror without the tail in your way.

Becky (Whatever are you doing, you weird wild man? Get out of there. I'm not a fur cap!)

Peggy Sue (Oh wow, Dad's really lost it this time! Try me, I'm a pretty blonde color. Go good with your tan!)

Michael & Scotty Richardson
Becky & Peggy Sue (The Golden Girls—Arf! Arf!)

TEDDY BEARS, COYOTES?

Made me think of the other day when we couldn't find one of our dogs big stuffed teddy bears—my wife volunteers at a local year-around rummage sale and is constantly dragging home stained, badly worn, or damaged stuffed animals that are not saleable. The dogs cart them about, and the bigger the teddy, the better they like them.

We noticed that a couple of the teddies had disappeared after being left out in the yard. Couldn't figure out what happened to them until the other day when I made my yearly foray into the woods behind the house to cut English ivy off the conifers. I found the badly mangled remains of the toys, apparent victims of the coyotes that populate this area. Well, I guess coyotes have to play too.

I admit the coyotes are beginning to make me a bit nervous. First they eat our cat, and now they steal dog toys. Anyone have an opinion as to whether or not they pose a threat to a sixty-pound golden retriever?

Becky (Hey if they mess with me I'll kick some coyote butt!)
Peggy Sue (I think they just want to have us for dinner!)

Michael & Scotty Richardson
Becky: The Red Scourge of Squirrels, Feline Track Coach
Peggy Sue: General Pixie, Lover of Every Creature

STRANGE—BALLS?

Following the thread on indestructible balls—our dogs showed *no* interest in them. As a matter of fact, Peggy Sue is afraid of them. Too hard.

However, a basketball we found in the woods (signed by Darryl Dawkins!) is one of their favorite toys. Tell Peggy Sue to "get Darryl Dawkins" and she jumps and rolls on the basketball.

Another favorite is her soccer ball. Short story here. We found a good soccer ball in the creek a year ago. Brought it home, threw it in the yard with the rest of the dog toys. I'm used to nudging the basketball out of the way of my power mower, didn't think twice about trying to nudge the soccer ball out of the way. Loud "braaaaaap" sound, soccer ball in thousands of pieces. Peggy Sue, standing over the carnage looking at me with a "why did you kill my soccer ball?" look on her face. For the next several days every time she went out, she brought a piece of the soccer ball in her mouth and looked at me with accusing eyes. I broke down and went to the store and paid $20.00 for a new soccer ball. Better than the guilt. She's better at guilt than my mother.

At any rate, they don't destroy these balls and, with a bit of work, can pack both of them around. Looks pretty funny, a dog with a basketball in their mouths! I wonder what Darryl Dawkins would think?

Becky (Who's Darryl Dawkins? Never heard of him. Is he a friend of Michael Jordan?)

Peggy Sue (No, you dummy. He's some real old guy like Dad. Probably plays basketball from his walker.)

Michael & Scotty Richardson
Becky: The Red Scourge of Squirrels, Feline Track Coach
Peggy Sue: General Pixie, Lover of Every Creature

A WAG IS A WAG?

Tail wagging is very expressive in my dogs. Here are some of my observations:

The *wahoo* wag. This is reserved for charging down a steep canyon, bounding over rocks, trees, bushes and other small impediments while rotating a very erect tail; using it for balance and as an aileron. Sometimes used while chasing small (or large) game.

The *cookie sweep* wag. Used by both dogs in synchronization while sitting on the kitchen floor, excitedly awaiting a goodie or two. For goodies they go to a sit position so quickly they make a resounding "thud" when their butts hit the floor.

The *happy dog hula* or full *body wiggle* wag. Reserved for happy occasions, such as greeting you after a long absence, like returning from the mailbox or returning from work each night. Also used in greeting new people and, much to his chagrin, the mailman.

The *oh hi* wag. Best demonstrated from a horizontal position, this is used when you enter a room occupied by a sleeping dog, usually consists of two or three "thumps" on the floor, then back to sleep.

The *get up, Dad* wag. This is the one where both dogs stand in the narrow hallway outside the bedroom when you try to sleep in, and bang their tails on both sides of the hall while "singing" loudly until you get up or get mad.

The *hummingbird quiver* wag. Only Becky does this one. This is done while laying prone on the down comforter at bed time. Just the last three inches of the tail moves in a fast fluttering motion. Nothing else moves, except the eyes, which fasten themselves upon my face with an "I love you so much you make my tail quiver" expression. This look would melt butter.

I've tried to teach this one to my wife, in vain, I fear.

Becky (My favorite is the wahoo wag! Let's go chase something like that deer I found yesterday below the house!)

Peggy Sue (My tail is pretty, as befits a sophisticate such as I. Looks like a great feathery plume. Makes a great duster!)

Michael & Scotty Richardson
Becky: The Red Scourge of Squirrels, Feline Track Coach
Peggy Sue: General Pixie, Lover of Every Creature

ONE MORE WAG TAIL

The *I did that on purpose* wag. This is the one following the resounding "splat" sound caused by sixty-five pounds of golden retriever traveling at a high rate of speed hitting a sliding glass door which is in the closed position.

In Becky's case, there was a squirrel sitting on the patio outside the door. After the one and only collision she had with the door (fast learner!), she was sort of hunkered down on her forelegs, a bit dazed, goofy grin on her face complete with teeth showing, tail wiggling rapidly back and forth with an "I meant that" look on her face. Now she just barks at them. I think she's cured of trying to chase them through the door.

Becky (Aw, Dad, you *know* how embarrassed I was about that. Did you have to tell the world?)

Peggy Sue (I ran into the door once, now I check with my paw to be sure it's open. You field dogs aren't that smart.)

Michael & Scotty Richardson
Becky: The Red Scourge of Squirrels, Feline Track Coach
Peggy Sue: General Pixie, Lover of Every Creature

MUSHROOM-STUFFED DOGS

Ah! November 22 and still no hard freeze! So off to the woods to check on the chanterelle situation. The area we are hunting today is muddy as can be; and of course, the girls are rolling in the mud. The only parts of the dogs recognizable are the eyes. All else is liberally coated in mud. This I can deal with. As a matter of fact, the mud makes the hair wet and sticky in the Hairmobile so you can open a window without wearing a surgical mask for a change. Once the mud dries in the van, we just take the air compressor and blow out the big stuff. The dogs, however, must be shampooed before they come in the house. They resemble moving dirt clods.

Isn't life with goldens great?

But they have learned that chanterelles are edible; although of inferior quality to deer scat! So now in addition to trying to outwit the commercial pickers, I have to fight my own dogs for the spoils of the forest! At least today the 'shrooms were plentiful. Both dogs ate their fill and we still brought home over fifty pounds. Tomorrow we feast! Happy Thanksgiving all!

Becky (I'm really really interested in those pies Mom is baking!)
Peggy Sue (I'm tired from all the mushroom picking and eating—*burrrrrrp*!)

Michael & Scotty Richardson
Becky: The Red Scourge of Squirrels, Feline Track Coach
Peggy Sue: General Pixie, Lover of Every Creature

TOO MUCH FUN?

I've decided that I want Michael and Scotty Richardson to adopt me. They just have too much fun in their household! More fun than we have here, for sure.

Scotty, you won't mind if we move in will you? Just me and two dogs and three cats (one of whom thinks he's a dog) . . .
I'm sure that Becky and Peggy Sue would be ecstatic to have five more friends to play with, and another human to pet them.

Do you do windows? No not MS Windows, this is a Mac household! No "clones" in this house! Well, we've got lots of room. And perhaps this would solve the problem of a dogsitter when we travel. We're headed for Mexico in January. And I've wanted another cat—as you may recall, Izzy; our last cat was eaten by the coyotes. Michael says "no more cats," but she'll cave in easily enough. She misses her kitty.
And I've wanted another dog—hmmmmm!

Becky (It's OK with me, but they need to know that *I'm the boss!*)
Peggy Sue (Oh boy, kitties! Will they play with me? I miss Izzy sitting on my head like a fur cap and biting my lips.)

Michael & Scotty Richardson
Becky: The Red Scourge of Squirrels, Feline Track Coach
Peggy Sue: General Pixie, Lover of Every Creature

WHY FIGHT A HOG?

In his books, *A Year in Provence* and *Toujours Provence*, Peter Mayle writes about his day-to-day life as a resident in France. Entertaining, informative, funny, and in one of the books (I forget which), he describes the art of truffle discovery as performed by pigs (the truffle-sniffer of choice) and dogs.

Just a quick sidebar (for those of you feeling deprived now that the OJ trial is history).
The main reason truffle hunters changed from hogs to dogs is quite simple.
The hog wants to *eat* the truffle. The dog is only interested in the treat he will receive from his handler for finding the truffle. Many is the story I have heard of a truffle hunter wrestling a hungry, angry four-hundred-pound hog for hypogeous fungi. Most of the time, the hog wins. Hence, the use of dogs.

Becky (I'm only sixty-five pounds of romping-stomping candy ass, but I can sure do battle for those chanterelles!)
Peggy Sue (I only fight for french fries.)

Michael & Scotty Richardson
Becky: The Red Scourge of Squirrels, Feline Track Coach
Peggy Sue: General Pixie, Lover of Every Creature

WATCHDOGS? HA!

Remember the recent thread on goldens as watch dogs? I had a chance to test my canine killers last night.

Got home from work at midnight. Opened the automatic garage door, which is so noisy it should wake the dead. Got out of the truck, slammed the door. (Bam!) Opened the door into the laundry room. Closed the door, firmly (slam!). Opened the door into the family room. There sound asleep, Becky, Peggy Sue, and my wife, Michael.

Peggy Sue on the futon with my wife, all four feet straight up in the air (Peggy Sue's, not Michael's) with her head stuffed under a pillow. Michael sound asleep, TV on, book in hand. Becky curled up on one of the LL Bean dog beds at Michael's feet. Total bliss! I stood there for at least a minute, listening to the snoring. Finally, I knelt down and put a hand on each dog. (I know better than to put a hand on a sleeping wife! I might lose it!) Even with my hand on them, they were slow to awaken. I believe the Bosnian army could have marched through the room, and they would have slept through it.

When they did awaken, they were smiling (the dogs, not my wife) as if they hadn't seen me for weeks. I wonder what would have happened had the person been a bad guy? So much for the protective watchdog stuff.

Becky (You cheated! You snuck up on us! I knew you were there, really!)
Peggy Sue (I sleep with my feet in the air so I can give that bad guy a karate kick! I thought you knew that!)

Michael & Scotty Richardson
Becky: The Red Scourge of Squirrels, Feline Track Coach
Peggy Sue: General Pixie, Lover of Every Creature

NOAH'S ARK? NAH! JUST SW WASHINGTON!

Holiday greetings; all! Just a word about our weather: *wet!* We are having record rainfall here in SW Washington, lots of flooding. Lots of folks suffering. But not my girls!

The meadow below our home is flooded, as is the creek. A meadow the girls romp through several times a week is now *swimming territory*! Wonderful dog fun, acres and acres of tall grass (eight feet) sticking out of the water. Just the right place for a *vigorous* game of fetch!

Down to the meadow in my Gore-Tex clothes, with a tennis racket and *ten* tennis balls in each pocket. Need a wide-load sign for my butt in this outfit.

The rain is being driven by 25 mph winds—*great* golden weather! Here I am, swatting tennis balls hundreds of feet out into the tall grass and water, two dogs fetching and searching *at full throttle*!

And then, I feel someone watching me. Looking behind me, I see three elderly ladies with large umbrellas fighting the wind and rain. The look on their faces says it all—and I realize how this must look. One crazy person in a camouflage coat, water pouring off me; tennis racket in hand and the nearest court *miles* away, shouting above the wind at two wet, *wild* beasts to "find the ball."

As soon as I smiled at the ladies and made eye contact, they sidled off to safety, never taking their eyes off me until they achieved a safe distance from this "Wackabilly" and his crazy canines. Hope I don't make the evening news. I did want to mention it's a good thing this breed wasn't around in Noah's time. Soon as they saw the water, he couldn't have kept them on the ark.

Becky (*Wahoooooooo!* Swat another *loooooong* one, Dad! I'll find it! I'll find it!)

Peggy Sue (Hey I like this game; but *whatever* did you feed that red field dog this morning? She's *nuts*!)

Michael & Scotty Richardson

Becky: The Red Scourge of Squirrels, Feline Track Coach

Peggy Sue: General Pixie, Lover of Every Creature

ROAD-HUNTING COWS?

The thread on interactive TV made me think of one of Becky's peculiarities.

She hunts cows. But only from a moving vehicle. When we have been up front and personal with cattle, she's not interested. I wondered if other goldens do this?

She won't sleep in a moving vehicle unless she is *totally* exhausted from one of our marathon hikes or a long day of fetching stuff out of the river. Instead, she spends her time looking out the windows of the Hairmobile for cows. She knows they generally live in open fields and pays special attention to these areas. If she spots a cow, she barks raucously until the cow is out of sight. Of course, she doesn't know the difference between horses and cows yet. We're working on that one. The other day, she spotted a couple of goats and got so confused she forgot to bark. As a general rule, Peggy Sue sleeps while we are en route. Wish I could.

Becky (*Cow alert! Cow alert!* Bark bark bark bark!)
Peggy Sue (Will you shut up? I'm trying for some shuteye here!)

Michael & Scotty Richardson
Becky: The Red Scourge of Squirrels, Feline Track Coach
Peggy Sue: General Pixie, Lover of Every Creature

DUMB DOG OWNER NEARLY CAUSES DISASTER

Almost lost my best friend today. If you read the news you know the flooding here in SW Washington has become very serious. The creeks and rivers are all at or above flood stage. Creeks that are normally harmless chuckling brooks become roaring torrents of water. Where usually there are sandy beaches the water is five feet up into brush and blackberry vines.

I went for a fifteen-mile hike today with my buddy Hank and my two goldens, Becky and Peggy Sue. Becky jumped into a creek when I wasn't watching closely enough. She has been in this stretch of water many times. Today, it almost killed her.

She was swept downstream by a raging current she couldn't swim against and went into a logjam. She was sucked under the logjam, struggling to keep her head above the water. As soon as I saw what was happening, I began tearing off my clothes in order to go in after her, which in retrospect, may have gotten me drowned as well as her. I had my coat, my pack, and one boot off when by some miracle of God she managed to give a mighty lurch which put her on top of one of the logs. She managed to get to the other shore and came upstream far enough to swim across to me, which was in itself a difficult feat. She had to hit a short section of shoreline, as there is nothing below this stretch but blackberry vines on both sides of the creek.

Both Becky and I are pretty shaken by this experience. I managed to get my left foot in the creek and walked the last eight miles home with a soggy stocking. Got a giant blister. Serves me right. It's reminding me I should have had Becky on a lead if there was any danger to her. I feel *really* dumb and, at the same time, extremely grateful that my *best* friend is lying at my feet, pooped out, as I write this. An experience like this reminds me just how much I love this dog. I doubt I could forgive myself if I lost her through my own stupidity.

Becky (Sorry, Dad, I thought I could swim against the current. I did it a week ago! Somebody put more water here!)
Peggy Sue (I told you not to swim today, you idiot field dog! You really scared us!)

Michael & Scotty Richardson
Becky: The Red Scourge of Squirrels, Feline Track Coach
Peggy Sue: General Pixie, Lover of Every Creature

ALL'S WELL—THANKS!

To all the marvelous folks on this list who responded with their support and stories after my post about Becky's near-drowning, thank you, thank you! I had no idea so many folks would respond. What a caring bunch!

Perhaps what the people and pets on this list need to do is to rent a *large* meeting place (Houston Astrodome?) and have a big family type meeting/reunion! We could bring *all* our dogs too, of course. I feel like part of a big supportive family.

Becky is fine, except for a fairly nasty cut on her front foot. She is hobbling about with a gauze-wrapped paw. I think she likes it! Of course, she has had "several" bad cuts on her pads in her four years with us and is used to being bandaged. She doesn't chew it or worry it in any way. I hold her paw and coo over her "owee" as if she were a child. Perhaps I'm nuts. But she *loves* the extra attention!

Both my girls got bathed and groomed last night, feet trimmed, etc. I feel so grateful we didn't lose one of them. Made the grooming even more enjoyable than usual, at least for me!

Thanks again for all your support. This is a *great* list! And these are great dogs!

Becky (Wanna hold my paw some more? Kiss it and make it better?)
Peggy Sue (Oh gad, are you ever neurotic! Typical field dog! Oh well, work it for all it's worth, that's my motto!)

Michael & Scotty Richardson
Becky: The Red Scourge of Squirrels, Feline Track Coach
Peggy Sue: General Pixie, Lover of Every Creature

WIND, RAIN, CAT POOP?

Hi all! Lots of private posts wondering how we fared. We are OK here in Vancouver, WA, but most of the neighbors didn't do as well. Big firs down on the neighbor's house. Lots of damage. I stood at the windows; heart in mouth watching our *wonderful* big firs whipping like twigs in the wind. Stress city!

Becky was her usual cool self, slept through most of the storm. Went out into the street during the worst of it (85 mph) and threw tennis balls for her. Boy, does an 85 mph wind ever increase my throwing range! Becky had to really boogie to catch those balls!

Peggy Sue (aka Nervous Nelly) didn't do as well. We finally had to give her a tranquilizer. She was pretty well-stoned when she needed to go potty. Michael accompanied her into the back yard and the wind whipped a plastic bag by her at warp nine or so—that did it! According to Peggy Sue, it was an obvious attempt on her life by an *attack sack*, and she preferred to hold it until all the plastic bags stopped moving.

So far this month, we have had flooding, more flooding, ice storms, and high winds. I heard a rumor (my dogs started this one) that it just *might* hail cat s*** next week. Golden heaven, eh?

Becky (Yawwwwnnnn! What storm? I'm sleepy!)
Peggy Sue *(Attack sack! Attack sack! Protect me, Mom!)*

Michael & Scotty Richardson
Becky: The Red Scourge of Squirrels, Feline Track Coach
Peggy Sue: General Pixie, Lover of Every Creature

VEHICLEPHOBIA? A CURE!

The day we picked up Becky from her temporary home (she was returned to the breeder at one year after a *really* bad couple of homes!), we literally had to force her into the VW Hairmobile. On the way home, she urinated all over herself and the van. She was terrified! If we drove under an overpass she would duck and cringe. We were told by our vet (who knows her history) that the only times she had ever been in a vehicle was to be dumped at another home—left with (not-too-kind) strangers.

It took a great deal of love, understanding, dog treats, toys, petting, etc., over a six-month period to get her to like riding in the Hairvagen.

But now, it seems she no longer fears being "dumped" somewhere when she gets into the car.

One really helpful thing was driving her to trails, woods, rivers, etc.

And letting her really romp with Peggy Sue. Soon, she began to *want* to go in the car!

At her present age of five, her favorite traveling pastime remains "cow hunting" which she can do for hours on end.

I would try making sure your dog equates your vehicle with *pleasure* even if you make some stops out of your way to entertain the dog. It worked for us!

Becky (O boy! Let's get in the Hairmobile and head for some mud! And maybe
I can bark at some cows!)

Peggy Sue (I really, really wish Mom would get me that Mercedes. I think I'd look good in it. VW vans are *too* common.)

Michael & Scotty Richardson
Becky: The Red Scourge of Squirrels, Feline Track Coach
Peggy Sue: General Pixie, Lover of Every Creature

POLITICS—NEWTICLES?

I just couldn't leave this alone. After signing off last night, I had a long political discussion with my dogs, Becky and the Pigger. So far they're the only ones who make any sense out of this current political environment.

They saw the article on "neuticles" and assured me it was a spelling error. They have information from a reliable source (Beavis and Butthead, hehhehheh) that the correct spelling is indeed "Newticles" and as we spoke *millions* of them are being manufactured to be used in place of campaign buttons for the GOP drive to the presidency in 1996. Soon, everyone will be pinning "Newticles" on their lapels. Collectors, better jump on this.

Someday these "Newticles" will be as highly sought after as your old "Tricky Dick" buttons. I sure hope this posting doesn't get me "blackballed"! :-)

Becky (Uhhhh geez, Dad, these are neat. But can't I just have my tennis balls back now?)
Peggy Sue (Hey, Mom, can we hang these from the rear view mirror of the
Hairmobile?)

P.S. In the event my dogs are wrong about this, perhaps we have hit upon a way to recognize other Golden_l list members at shows? :-)

Michael & Scotty Richardson
Becky: The Red Scourge of Squirrels, Feline Track Coach
Peggy Sue: General Pixie, Lover of Every Creature

NEWTICLES II

Thank you for waiting two weeks after I was spayed to write this post. I can finally laugh again.

Can we put the Newticles on wires on headbands, ala SNL and Belushi.

How about on the "mortar boards" of students graduating with a degree in political sciences?

Becky (I *still* want my tennis balls back!)
Peggy Sue (Will my bark get deeper if I wear these?)

Michael & Scotty Richardson
Becky: The Red Scourge of Squirrels, Feline Track Coach
Peggy Sue: General Pixie, Lover of Every Creature

ITCHING, BATHING?

Our four-year-old golden has had sensitive skin, and therefore, the vet has given us a special shampoo to use called "ETIDERM." The problem is that after her bath she itches constantly for a day or so. This is after following the directions and after the day of itching she seems ok.

Are there some suggestions or ideas as to what the problem might be? I appreciate any help.

We have had constant itching problems with Peggy Sue for all her life. We've tried every shampoo known to man or dog, been to the vets, etc., and nothing worked until we took the following advice from a gentleman selling skin products at the Portland Bench Show. I hope some of you experienced breeders will tell us if there is any harm in this solution to itching.

Here goes: Rinse your dog in a solution of one-half cup of common white vinegar to one gallon of water. Leave this on for about ten minutes, then rinse thoroughly. According to this gentleman, it rids the skin of bacteria which can cause hot spots, etc. The next step is optional, but it improves the dog's coat (and smell!) and that is to use a show rinse that is left on the coat, not rinsed out. Just towel or blow dry the dog, leaving the rinse in.

It *really* worked on Peggy Sue. I had much doubt about this process, but as I said, *It worked*.

Experts, please advise!

Becky (I'm a field dog. I'm tough! I only get staph infections! Scratch itch, itch)

Peggy Sue (I don't care if I smell like a kosher pickle, I don't itch!)

Michael & Scotty Richardson
Becky: The Red Scourge of Squirrels, Feline Track Coach
Peggy Sue: General Pixie, Lover of Every Creature

HAPPINESS IS—

Doing electrical work through a small hole in the floor, standing on one's head, with your chief electrical inspector (aka Becky) lying against you, nose in hole, making *sure* you know what you're doing!

Becky (Uhhhhhh are you *sure* you turned that circuit off?)
Peggy Sue (I dunno what's in that hole, but it *really* makes me nervous!)

Michael & Scotty Richardson
Becky: The Red Scourge of Squirrels, Feline Track Coach
Peggy Sue: General Pixie, Lover of Every Creature

VACUUM CLEANER PHOBIA?

As far as Becky is concerned, the vacuum is a lovable friend. Even though it sucks. So far haven't found *anything* that scares the s*** out of her! While hiking today, she was jumped on (literally) by a Dalmatian. The fight was on! So now I'm nursing a sore ankle from jumping in and breaking things up. No harm done to either dog.
Just a lot of huffing, puffing, and chest bumping.

Becky (I don't take *no* s*** from spotted dogs! I coulda whipped him!)
Peggy Sue (I don't fight for any reason. Except perhaps, cookies!)

Michael & Scotty Richardson
Becky: The Red Scourge of Squirrels, Feline Track Coach
Peggy Sue: General Pixie, Lover of Every Creature

STUFFED TOYS ARE WOOBIES?

So all this time my girls stuffed toys have been "woobies" eh? What I learn from this list! The girls love stuffed toys! Becky has been known to stroll around the house with new toys in her mouth for *hours*, wagging, whining, talking. Usually, the "new" wears off the toy after a day or so, although the girls each have their favorites. Peggy Sue knows how to get a toy away from Becky anytime she wants it. If Becky has something Peggy Sue wants, Peggy Sue will find another "woobie" and shake it, talk to it, pounce on it, etc., until Becky *can't stand it* and jumps in to snatch the toy from the Pigger. At this point Peggy Sue leaps on the toy Becky dropped and spirits it from the room. This always leaves Becky with an "oh no, I've been had" look on her face. At this point the *great chase* is on! If Becky gets the toy back, Peggy Sue simply repeats the process.

Becky (Gimme that! That's the one I want—whoops! Now I want *that* one!)
Peggy Sue (Bait and switch works on that dummy field dog every time! I should have sold used cars!)

Michael & Scotty Richardson
Becky: The Red Scourge of Squirrels, Feline Track Coach
Peggy Sue: General Pixie, Lover of Every Creature

PUPPY CRYING AT NIGHT?

Just a couple of additions to a lot of really good suggestions. Peggy Sue was only seven weeks when we brought her home, and from the first night, she was with us in the bedroom. She was in a crate with a hot water bottle (wrapped in a towel) and a ticking windup travel clock. This was at the suggestion of her breeder. It seemed to work well; we had few problems with being kept awake.

Coincidentally, Becky came to us almost at the same time as Peggy Sue, but she was a rescue dog over a year old. She had never been allowed in someone's house, let alone the bedroom. Both dogs sleep in our bedroom and are allowed on the king-sized bed while we read for a while before the lights go out. They *love* this cuddle time on the down comforter. At lights out, they both sleep next to us on the floor on their own beds. Becky is *never* more than arm's length from me. We wouldn't have it any other way.

Becky (Hey, Dad, turn up the electric blanket a bit, would you? *Mmmmmm* that's just right—!)
Peggy Sue (*Zzzzzzzzzzzzzzz*)

Michael & Scotty Richardson
Becky: The Red Scourge of Squirrels, Feline Track Coach
Peggy Sue: General Pixie, Lover of Every Creature

IT AIN'T ALL FUN—

She's back from the doctor's office; here's what he came up with. She has an elevated level of E. coli in her stool (the vet asked if we had fed her anything from jack-in-the box restaurants :-}). His first thought was giardia, which is common in this area, because we run our dogs in places frequented and inhabited by beavers. No sign of Giardia, however. Her temperature was a bit elevated (102.6), but the doc said that's probably due to stress from the examination. He put her on antibiotics (metronidazole 1000 mg daily for five days) and a prescription dog food (Hill's Canine I/D) for a week. She is eating the prescription food (canned stuff!) and does appear to have a little more life in her this morning. She did wake me up singing and wiggling this morning (her, not me!) and was packing a toy in her mouth, something she didn't do at all yesterday.

We mentioned some of the possibilities suggested by folks on this list (Addison's, etc.), and the doc's comment was: "let's separate out the horses before we look for zebras!" I like this particular vet, have seen him for years, he's knowledgeable, and has an excellent manner with my dogs. And me! If this doesn't clear up Peggy Sue's problem in a few days, he will do the blood tests but doesn't think there is any point in it unless her condition worsens.

Our sincere thanks to all of you who so kindly privately posted helpful hints and support to us last night. Sorry about treating this as a crisis— but these are our babies!

Becky (Hey why can't I have some of that canned food! What the hey is going on here? Food strike! I'm not gonna eat this old dry junk—oh well, I guess I will—)

Peggy Sue (I feel really crappy, don't push me, Becky—I'll show you ALL my teeth!)

Michael & Scotty Richardson
Becky: The Red Scourge of Squirrels, Feline Track Coach
Peggy Sue: General Pixie, Lover of Every Creature

SMELLY DOG?

I'm writing for a friend who hasn't come into the "cyberspace" generation yet. They have a three-year-old dog who has a terrible body (not teeth) odor. They bathe it, but within twenty-four to forty-eight hours, the smell returns. They also say the dog is very itchy.

Ok—here goes. I *know* this sounds silly, but try vinegar. Peggy Sue had chronic skin problems, hot spots, bad smell, etc. All until we ran across a kind expert at a dog show, and he gave us these instructions:

Bathe dog well in a good dog shampoo (we use Ring 5).
Rinse thoroughly, get all the soap out mix one-half cup of white vinegar to a gallon of water, wet the dog well with this potion, and leave on for ten minutes.
Rinse the dog well.
The last step is optional: Use a good show rinse of the type you leave in the coat and towel dry the dog.

Peggy Sue's BO and skin irritations are history at this point. It's been a couple of months now, no problems. We have done this every three weeks or so.
Apparently, the vinegar kills bacteria on the dog much as it does in cooking and canning of foods. I *know* it sounds silly—but it worked!

Becky (I never smell bad. I even liked the odor of that *dead gopher* I rolled in the other day!)

Peggy Sue (I smell like a kosher pickle that's been perfumed!)

Michael & Scotty Richardson
Becky: The Red Scourge of Squirrels, Feline Track Coach
Peggy Sue: General Pixie, Lover of Every Creature

THE FECAL GOURMET?

All this talk of "poopsicles" prompted this post. We also have the pleasure of living with a lawn-taco connoisseur. Peggy Sue likes *nothing* better than her *own* warm, steaming turf tootsie rolls. Only her own, mind you. Wouldn't *think* of eating another dogs predigested leftovers. During her recent digestive problem the vet put her on a prescription food, some canned stuff that stunk even *before* we ran it through the dog. I swear we thought we would need a doggy chiropractor due to the positions she twisted herself into during her delivery of these tasty morsels. The only way you beat her to these "turf treats" was to practically hold the pooper-scooper under her.

Our dog sitter summed it up when we asked him how he did with the poop-eater during his last stay. Peggy Sues apre' toilet habit is particularly nauseating for him. "I got 'em all while they were still steaming" was his reply. Good man!

Becky (I like horse poop. The shape is similar to my tennis balls!)
Peggy Sue (MMMMMMM! Lookie here what I found *right* behind me—)

Michael & Scotty Richardson
Becky: The Red Scourge of Squirrels, Feline Track Coach
Peggy Sue: General Pixie, Lover of Every Creature

A "FLUKE" PERHAPS? OR NOT

Greetings, all! Thought I'd run this by the group, nobody except golden people could possibly understand this.

We rented a video Monday night and watched it with our dogs. The video was

Fluke. Some of you are familiar with it; we rented it because someone on this list recommended it.

The girls were both interested in it, but Becky was absolutely riveted to the screen. For those of you unfamiliar with the video, the story revolves around a stray dog. There are two scenes in particular Becky showed a *lot* of interest in. One scene showed the dog tied up outside in the rain and mud. The other scene showed a family inside a house, with the dog outside looking in. Many of you are aware that Becky is a rescue dog, a victim of a bad first year. She spent most of her first year in a small yard with no human contact.

OK, all you canine pop psychologists, here's the question: How much do dogs remember? Could they have flashbacks? (No, they don't do drugs!) Do they have nightmares?

Any research been done on this? The reason I ask is because Becky hid behind my recliner after the movie. She seemed very upset. Then we had to pull

Becky *out from under our bed* this morning. She had crawled as far under as she could go and was *very* wedged under the bed. No way could she have gotten out without help. This is completely atypical of her. Is it possible scenes in the movie triggered bad memories?

Becky (No way I want to go back to that sort of life! Next time rent a happier video. That was sooooooo depressing!)

Peggy Sue (I liked it. But parts of it were a bit boring. And I'm too *round* to get under the bed!)

Michael & Scotty Richardson
Becky: The Red Scourge of Squirrels, Feline Track Coach
Peggy Sue: General Pixie, Lover of Every Creature

USFS VS. CANINE FREEDOM?

I know this is going to tweak some noses, but I just have to offer my two cents on this business of the USFS banning dogs in wilderness areas or USFS land in general.

Michael and I have worked closely with the USFS and the BLM in Oregon and Washington because of our mycological avocation. As many of you know there is a *problem* with commercial mushroom picking in our areas. One thing we have learned is that the USFS is highly influenced by powerful lobby groups, such as ORV clubs, horse clubs, organizations with clout, such as the Mazamas, Sierra Club, etc. Most, if not all of these organizations, are primarily interested in their own continued usage of our forests. Not yours or mine. If you are vocal enough, and visible enough, you will likely catch some one's attention for your cause.

Because there is no money to be gained from Mushroom hobbyists, even though we were using the forests for forty years before the commercial pickers, we have come out a distant second in the fight for forest privileges. There is little income to be gained from hobbyists to fatten the USFS and BLM wallets. The commercial pickers hire lobbyists and their own scientists (much as the timber companies) to further their own interest in the forests—money.

Here's my point (finally)—as long as there is *no* organized voice for allowing our pets in the wilderness and on the trails used by hikers and horses, we won't even be considered. You can take this one to the bank—unless there is organized outrage, your dogs *will* be banned from the forests. I would hate to see this happen. My dogs have always accompanied us on our hikes. We do not run them off leash in areas we know will be heavily used by others. But there are thousands of miles of trails around here which are little used, and my girls are allowed to *run free.*

Yes, I have met people with problem dogs; had one almost take my leg off last summer. But 90 percent of the people we meet on trails with dogs either off or on lead are courteous and not problematic. It is a mistake to hike with dogs off-lead in areas used heavily by horses. Tell that to the moron who doesn't care if his dog causes an accident. As in all things, 5 percent of the dog owners cause 95 percent of the problems. No, I don't know the answer to this, but I'm all too familiar with the problem. Anyone offering any solutions out there?

Becky (Not go hiking? How will I collect ticks? I love to run!)
Peggy Sue (I never leave Dad's heels, but I sure do like the woods!)

PS
I posted this yesterday, but it never showed up. So if it shows up twice, I'm sorry. Blame the electronic cyberspooks.

Michael & Scotty Richardson
Becky: The Red Scourge of Squirrels, Feline Track Coach
Peggy Sue: General Pixie, Lover of Every Creature

RAWHIDE, ETC.

Hi all,

Just curious—can someone enlighten me as to the dangers associated with giving your golden rawhide to chew on? Several of you have referred to this. We give Winnie rawhide toys, i.e. big sticks, pretzel shapes, etc., because she snubs her Nylabones and it's the only thing that seems to help when she is in her "bitey" moods.

Our vet is *dead* set against rawhide. Or cow hooves; pig ears, etc. About the only approved items on his chew list are the boiled bones, Nylabones, and other items of that ilk. Rawhide chews have caused him too many emergency surgeries by causing intestinal obstruction.
Anyway, why would you want your dog to chew on anything as *disgusting* as pig ears, cow hooves (yech they stink) when there are other things available? Cow hooves cause slimy rugs, slimy dogs, and leave areas that look as if slugs crawled on them. If you don't have slugs in your areas, you're lucky. How about snails? Same slimy yech stuff.

Becky (Well, *you* may think they're disgusting. I don't! Now beets, they're disgusting.)
Peggy Sue (I prefer poop, anyway. Softer, easier to digest. But it's *always* outside. How 'bout bringing some in? It's cold out there.)

Michael & Scotty Richardson
Becky: The Red Scourge of Squirrels, Feline Track Coach
Peggy Sue: Pixie, Lover of Every Creature, Fecal Gourmet

RETURN FROM YUCATAN VACATION

We're back! And as most of you know, the Portland/Vancouver areas of Oregon/Washington are severely flooded. Fortunately, we are OK here, as we sit on a hill above the creek. Where usually there is a small creek, now we have three-fourths of a mile of water behind us. The trail we run the girls on is usually twenty feet above the water. It is now submerged. The damage is unbelievable. I work at the marine terminals on the Columbia River. The terminals are partly under water; the electrical equipment is submerged.

We cannot return to work until the water recedes. When it does, we will work around the clock until things are back online. There are golden retrievers in the Yucatan! Probably the most well-cared for dog we saw on our trip was a gorgeous blonde golden, walking about a primitive village consisting primarily of houses made of sticks with palm-thatch roofs. This dog appeared to be a status symbol!

The temperatures were in the 80s and low 90s as it is early spring there. But the summers are hot, 120 degrees not unusual. Seems severe for a golden retriever? There are dogs everywhere in the Yucatan, usually mixed breeds. While eating in restaurants on the beaches of the Caribbean, the village dogs walk through for a handout! Michael and I were spotted right away as a soft touch, and several of the village dogs returned to share both our breakfasts and dinner. No one pays much attention to these dogs.

They don't like to be petted or touched. Just fed! In a small village near the ruins at Coba, we observed pigs, chickens, turkeys, goats, sheep, dogs, cats, burros, and villagers living in perfect harmony. There are no fences, everything runs loose. Sometimes this is a problem as there are many critters wandering about the roads. And the roads are narrow and have little or no shoulder, just a sharp drop into the jungle.

For as many dogs as there are in the area, there is almost no barking. The dogs are not territorial and wander about at will. We only observed one dog tied up, and that was at a mostly American village/resort. And the poor dog was barking his head off!

This trip was wonderful! We would highly recommend this area to anyone who is interested in ruins or snorkeling in wonderful clear bays through coral reefs. Or just hang on the beaches and get a tan. Swimming in the Caribbean is a treat for us, as the Pacific Ocean here is too cold to be comfortable.

The food was wonderful! You must be careful what you eat and drink, however, as the tap water is usually bad. We had no problems finding pure water; there is bottled water available at every small grocery store in every village.

Becky and Peggy Sue were ecstatic at our return, what a golden greeting! They were a bit house-bound as the dog sitter is afraid to run them much.

Michael will be making the girls new beds from some serapes we purchased in a small village for $4.00. These are nicely made cotton blankets, very heavy, measuring about four feet wide and seven feet long. Great bargains!

Becky (Boy, does your luggage smell funny, Dad. Where the heck were you, anyway?)

Peggy Sue (Yeah, you smell like a burro. Must be the fine wool in the serapes you brought home!)

Michael & Scotty Richardson
Becky: The Red Scourge of Squirrels, Feline Track Coach
Peggy Sue: Pixie, Lover of Every Creature, Fecal Gourmet

RED DOG GUILT TRIP?

Anybody else out there with a golden retriever good at laying guilt trips? My poor Becky is really on my case. First we left Becky and Peggy Sue with their favorite dog sitter while we vacationed in Mexico. They were *so* happy to see us when we got back! But then—as most of you know we have had *serious* flooding here in Washington and Oregon. I work on the waterfront. When we returned from vacation, there was no waterfront. Our huge waterfront cranes as well as all the buildings, high voltage vaults, etc. suffered severe water damage. In order to get things operational, I have worked (at least) twelve-hour days seven days a week since our return.

Becky is letting me *know* that perhaps the vacation was acceptable, but this business of not being home at all except to sleep is cutting into our quality dog time!

The other night I sat in my huge recliner which, except for our bed, is Becky's favorite place on earth. She sat with me in the chair for a bit, fidgeted, and then left me to lie behind the chair. Every time we made eye contact, she had that *you don't love me anymore* look on her face. No amount of coaxing got her back on my lap. However, potato chips worked. I have to hand it to her—the only individual capable of making me feel more guilty about anything is my mother. Perhaps they have been collaborating?

Another week or so and things will be back to normal, I hope. We can't even let the girls swim in the creek below the house as the sewers flooded (nasty!), and there is unmentionable stuff everywhere. Time should heal all, eh?

Michael & Scotty Richardson
Becky: The Red Scourge of Squirrels, Feline Track Coach
Peggy Sue: Pixie, Lover of Every Creature, Fecal Gourmet

CONNISEWERS?

Scene: A rainy, windy, muddy (in other words, typical Oregon weather) day on the trail below our house. We are now in the meadow which was recently flooded, off-lead.

Becky (Hey, Pigger, how about that post on the Golden-L suggesting dogs knew about wines?)

Peggy Sue (Whine? I'm not whining!)

Becky (Not whining, you dolt, *wine* which is something good to drink, I guess.)

Peggy Sue (Never heard of it. But look! A dead fish, left from the flood! And it's really raunchy!)

Becky (Cool! Good find! Now—should we roll in it first and then eat it?)

Peggy Sue (Hey it's mine, I saw it first! I'm gonna roll in it!)

Becky (Uhhhhh—I dunno, you know how royally pissed Dad gets when we do that.)

Peggy Sue (I'm going for it!) Roll, roll, roll! (Boy, that smells great! Now let's eat it! Wait! Whatever is that high wailing noise?)

Becky (Ooops! It's Dad! And he looks really unhappy—I'm outa here!)

Peggy Sue (Me too!)

Becky (Wait! There's some deer poop here! I think we have *just* enough time to scoop this gourmet delight before Dad catches us! MMMMMM!)

Becky (Life is good, eh?)

Peggy Sue (Yeah, life is a hoot! Look out, here he comes! I bet we're gonna get another smelly bath—yuk! I really prefer this dead fish smell.)

Becky (I know, I know—there's no understanding these humans.)

Michael & Scotty Richardson
Becky: The Red Scourge of Squirrels, Feline Track Coach
Peggy Sue: Pixie, Lover of Every Creature, Fecal Gourmet

BROKEN MOLARS, DENTAL BANDITS

Well, just wanted to thank all of you who e-mailed us privately with information regarding Peggy Sue's *very expensive* broken molar.

The general consensus seems to be that the prices we are being quoted are *outrageous* to say the least. It has even been suggested we could afford to fly the Pigger to LA to have the procedure done, (first class, with cocktails!) and still save money! Guess the Portland area must have better dentists for dogs? Is that why these prices are so high?

Another person suggested that the prices reflected the high cost of Vaseline in this area. I agree with that one, for sure!

So far, most folks agree it's better in the long run to just pull the tooth if you are not showing the dog. Less complications.

I am awaiting a call from the doggy dentist; I will attempt to negotiate with this bandit on the basis of prices you have quoted from other parts of the country.

The moral of this story is: don't break your tooth in this part of the country.

Becky (Why did you take my hard chewies away? I've got goooood teeth!)
Peggy Sue (Can I fly United? I like the airline treats you bring me when you fly on that airline. Eagle snacks! Yummy!)

Michael & Scotty Richardson
The Golden Girls
Becky: The Red Scourge of Squirrels, Feline Track Coach
Peggy Sue: Pixie, Lover of Every Creature, Fecal Gourmet

TEETH, FRENCH OARS?

Update on the Pigger's tooth—after minimal negotiations with the best dental vet in the area (he teaches at the veterinary school) he has agreed to pull the tooth for $130.00. It's about a two-hour surgery, he said. He agrees with those on this list that pulling is the answer, as in his experience root canals last about five years and then you will have more problems, so why put the critter through this twice?

(Becky) Hey great walk this morning, eh? I really liked the part when you found that groovy dead fish again, Peggy Sue!
(Peggy Sue) Yeah, well I marked it pretty well the other day. Figured I could find it again.
(Becky) Dad sure was right on top of us this morning, though, think he suspected something?
(Peggy Sue) Probably. But he's only fast for the first one hundred yards or so anyway.
(Becky) Too bad you only had time to get one shoulder in that fish.
(Peggy Sue) Yeah, I didn't really get as smelly as I wanted. Better than nothing though.
(Becky) Dad said it isn't bad enough to bathe you. That's a plus!
(Peggy Sue) Yeah, but PPPPPPP—UUUUUUU this stuff he sprayed on me stinks!
(Becky) What the heck is that perfumey junk, anyway?
(Peggy Sue) Dunno, but it has something to do with foreign boats.
(Becky) How do you figure?
(Peggy Sue) Well, Mom says I smell like a French oar.
(Becky) Guess she must have done some rowing, eh?

Michael & Scotty Richardson
The Golden Girls
Becky: The Red Scourge of Squirrels, Feline Track Coach
Peggy Sue: Pixie, Lover of Every Creature, Fecal Gourmet

BECKY—PUSSYCAT PATROL

The thread on feline trespassers reminded me of a funny story.

When we moved to this home, we still had Izzy, our (and Peggy Sue's) cat.

In the old 'hood, Izzy, with a little help from her two golden friends, had whipped every other cat attempting to cross her territory. Things were good. Top cat.

Then we moved. The territorial lines were not clear. The previous owners had no cats. The neighbors did. Trouble was brewing. We sensed it. Izzy immediately set out to establish her new territory.

The neighbors had a large woodpile where their cats would languish away the sunny afternoons. Unfortunately, it was within one hundred yards of our yard.

Izzy had a problem with this. So off she would trundle to the woodpile, fixin' to kick a little a**. Much yowling, screaming, hissing, etc., would emanate from the area. Due to the fact there were four neighbor cats and only one Izzy, her odds were poor.

But fear not! Becky, friend of Izzy, foe of *any* other cat, would hear the cacophony and run to me, bouncing, up and down, as if to say: "CAT FIGHT! CAT FIGHT! LEMMMEEEEE GO GETTTT 'EMMMMM!"

Of course, Becky was trained not to chase the neighbor kitties. But that was her buddy over there getting her little kitty butt kicked. So "go help Izzy," I would tell her.

Off like a shot goes the Red Dog Cat Rescue! Watching the action that ensued at the woodpile was always great entertainment. Neighbor cats spurting out from all over, heading into the woods! Izzy standing with back arched watching them run, as if to say "I *told* you I am the queen of the 'hood, and my friend would be here!" Becky is somewhere in the woods, in hot pursuit.

Needless to say, even though Izzy fell prey to the coyotes and resides at the Rainbow Bridge where she patiently awaits her golden buddies—we still don't have a cat problem in this yard!

So for a small gratuity, perhaps you people with cat trouble could hire the "Red Scourge of Squirrels, Feline Track Coach" for a few days. Results guaranteed!

Seriously, please go easy on the cats and their owners. Cats do what cats want to do. It is very difficult, if not impossible to train cats to stay in a yard. We loved our cat as well as our dogs. Remember how you feel about your dogs and that most cat owners (us included) can be just as passionate about their cats.

Try using the commercially available cat repellents. They worked for us, and they don't harm the cats or create a neighborhood problem.

Becky (Cat? Where? *Gottaaaaa chassseee 'emmmmm!* Cats just have *no* respect!)

Peggy Sue (I just sniff 'em. Chasing is toooooo common. But after all, you *are* a field dog.)

Michael & Scotty Richardson
The Golden Girls
Becky: The Red Scourge of Squirrels, Feline Track Coach
Peggy Sue: Pixie, Lover of Every Creature, Fecal Gourmet

PEGGY SUE'S CAT BOX

Becky (Hey, Pigger, what'cha doing with that shovel?)

Pigger (Shoveling sand, what's it look like?)

Becky (Yeah, I see that, but *why* are you shoveling all that sand into the backyard?)

Pigger (Well—I'm makin' me a cat box.)

Becky (A cat box? What for?)

Pigger (I was reading the Golden-L the other day, and they were talking about cats, and I got to thinking. You're always running all the cats out of the yard; you big red dummy. I miss my snacks! If I make a nice enough kitty-litter area, perhaps I can lure them back.)

Becky (You can't talk about cats or make scatological references on the Golden-L; you know.)

Pigger (Sorry. You're right. Wanna help me shovel?)

Becky (Sure. Gotta admit; you're right about the snacks. Think this'll work?)

Pigger (Dunno. Hope so. Shoveling gives me an appetite.)

Michael & Scotty Richardson
The Golden Girls
Becky:; The Red Scourge of Squirrels, Feline Track Coach
Peggy Sue: Pixie, Lover of Every Creature, Fecal Gourmet

HORROR IN THE WOODS?

Had to jump on this—the most *vicious* I have ever seen Becky was on a hike through a recently burned forest area. Down the trail we come—hiking merrily, happily along, sniffing the spring flowers—*and then!* (Dragnet music here) Becky goes ballistic! I mean *totally berserk!* Barking, slavering, spittle flying! I'm sure we are in mortal danger. Must be another bear—or the Sasquatch. I continue, at a snail's pace, awaiting my impending doom. Peggy Sue, BTW is not reacting at all. Strange. Becky is hesitant to follow me, but does so—all the time warning me that we are all *about to die!*
And then—I spot what she is soooo upset about. It's a *killer stump!* An old, burned out snag that is obviously about to spring upon us!
So I did what any normal person would do at this stage of the danger. I ran down the trail lickety brindle, Becky the Brave at my heels. And sure 'nuff, we got away from that killer stump. But Becky wasn't happy until it was well behind us and I assured her it was OK.
Trust your dog's instincts? Hmmmmm. I'll think on that one.

Becky (I'm telling you, if we weren't so darn fast on the downhills—we were toast!)
Pigger (What the heck is *wrong* with that red dog? Now, big cardboard boxes—that's scary!)

Michael & Scotty Richardson
The Golden Girls
Becky: The Red Scourge of Squirrels, Feline Track Coach
Peggy Sue: Pixie, Lover of Every Creature, Fecal Gourmet

PIGGER'S DENTAL SURGERY

This is the big day. As I write this Peggy Sue is in surgery to have her carnisical (sp?) molar removed, as it was badly broken. She was terrified this morning when we had to leave her at this strange vet's office. We are anxiously awaiting some word from the vet as to her condition. He said the procedure takes about two hours, as the tooth usually has to be split into pieces in order to remove it.

Becky is beside herself, she and the Pigger are *never* separated. She mopes about, leaning on me and plopping her head in my lap. I know just how she feels.

Please think good thoughts for the Pigger. Don't know what we'd do without her ROOOO—ROOOOOing and other cute antics!

Becky (What have you done with my friend? I *really* miss her.)
Peggy Sue ()

Michael & Scotty Richardson
The Golden Girls
Becky: The Red Scourge of Squirrels, Feline Track Coach
Peggy Sue: Pixie, Lover of Every Creature, Fecal Gourmet

PIGGER IS HOME!

Pigger's oral surgery went well and she is now home with us! Thanks to all of you who thought good thoughts for us. She is a sweetie; we worry too much, I guess.

All the folks at the vet's office fell in love with her. But home was on her mind when Michael picked her up! She even slipped her collar trying to get to Michael. So, soft food and lots of extra spoiling for the next several days. Think she'll do well on Haagen-Dazs ice cream?

Becky (What's all the fuss over the Pigger? Why don't you soak MY treats to soften them?)

Peggy Sue (My mouth hurts—but I bet I could get used to all this extra good treatment! Hey, Mom, bring me some more ice cream, hurry it up, will ya?)

Michael & Scotty Richardson
The Golden Girls
Becky: The Red Scourge of Squirrels, Feline Track Coach
Peggy Sue: Pixie, Lover of Every Creature, Fecal Gourmet

DESTROY THE ENEMY!

Apollo finally won the battle. We usually leave him in the downstairs hallway behind baby gates during the day. In the hallway is a louver door closet in which is the hated Hoover. We came home the other day to find that he had somehow managed to get the doors open, probably by pawing them till they swung open. He found his enemy, examined it and chewed off the electric plug. I came home to find the dismembered plug sitting by his side, Apollo with an expression of satisfaction on his mug.

A friend had a similar situation with their Doberman who literally *killed* the $500.00 Snapper lawn mower they just purchased. Unbelievable amount of damage when they left it out of the garden shed and went to the store. Found the dog sitting staring at it, somewhat exhausted, with a satisfied look on her face. The enemy is conquered!

Becky (Why all the fuss? If it sucks or blows, I love it!)
Peggy Sue (OK, but have you seen the look in that lawn mowers eyes? I dunno about that sucker.)

Michael & Scotty Richardson
The Golden Girls
Becky: The Red Scourge of Squirrels, Feline Track Coach
Peggy Sue: Pixie, Lover of Every Creature, Fecal Gourmet

SPRING IS IN THE (H)AIR

I'm so choked up as I write this. No, I'm not overcome by emotion. Read on. And rest assured, I will not use the word "poop" in this post.

Ah spring! The birds are singing, my wife has planted her yearly quota of bulbs, the grass is green—and the girls are blowing their coats. Achhhhh!

Hair in my food, hair on my clothes, hair in my mouth, everywhere but on my head, where I could use it.

Today—today I made a *real* mistake. Off to the garden store via the freeway with the new 70 mph speed limit (close to wide open for a VW van). Both the girls happily riding along. Becky hunting cows, her favorite traveling sport. The sun comes out. It warms up in the Hairmobile. I open the window—*mistake!*" WHOOOOOSSSHHHH! We all disappear in a cloud of dog hair! I can barely see to drive! We weren't expecting warm weather. Didn't expect to open any windows. Left the surgical masks home. Surgical masks are an essential accessory for golden owners who drive with the windows open during coat-blowing time. Sure it looks a little funny driving along wearing these things. So what? I wasn't handsome to begin with. Stare, you idiots. You don't have the pleasure of owning two (very) hairy goldens.

I pull into the right lane and slow to 55 mph and close the window. The hair settles. Folks behind us are wondering what that huge cloud was emanating from that VW van. Probably just another engine fire. Sure engine fires are annoying but VW vans just do that once in a while. You learn to live with it.

We are home safely now, I will once again break out the air compressors and blow out most of the hair from the Hairvagen. Life goes on. If neither of us is hospitalized with a hairball, it wasn't such a bad day!

Becky (Whoa! Where the heck did all that hair come from? Peggy Sue, are you shedding again?)
Peggy Sue (Don't blame me, you idiot. Probably came from Dad. Look at his head. I think the rest of his hair just blew off.)

Michael & Scotty Richardson
The Golden Girls
Becky: The Red Scourge of Squirrels, Feline Track Coach
Peggy Sue: Pixie, Lover of Every Creature, Fecal Gourmet

PEGGY SUE—SEIZURE!

I know this isn't the medical hotline, and to those of you who object to this use of the list, I apologize. However, this isn't an emergency, and I have read many postings on this subject before. I just hoped we would never need this sort of advice; but I fear we do.

Peggy Sue suffered a small seizure of some kind this a.m. I was awakened by

Michael shouting, "Scotty, there's something wrong with Peggy Sue," in a hysterical voice. Bad way to awaken.

Just as I crawled out of bed, Michael and Becky came down the hall with Peggy Sue in tow. Peggy Sue was staggering like a drunken sailor and shaking uncontrollably. I sat on the floor, and Peggy Sue crawled into my lap. I held her and stroked her and crooned to her in a low voice; pretty soon, the shaking stopped. After three to five minutes, she reached up and kissed me, and I checked her pupils, which were somewhat dilated. Another five minutes and she was OK. I helped her up; she went straight to the kitchen and drank a lot of water. From this point on, perhaps fifteen minutes after the initial episode, she appeared normal in every way.

Less than two weeks ago, she had a complete physical, normal and healthy in every way. There is *no* way she ate anything in the last three days we don't know about. She was pronounced healthy by the vet who pulled her tooth a week and a half ago. The tooth surgery seems to have healed nicely and is not bothering her anymore. No swelling, nothing, I checked the incision this morning.

We have seen these seizures before with our now "over the bridge" Doberman, but she was ten before these started. Pigger is only four and a half years old. I also know that in most cases, these seizures are over long before you can get the dog to a vet, particularly on a weekend as this is a Saturday.

Any and all advice is welcomed and solicited. I know many of you have had similar frightening experiences. Please help us figure out a path to take.

Our Doberman took phenobarbital for the seizures. Is this a way to go? Or just help Peggy Sue through the seizure and wait and see?

BTW, Becky alerted Michael to Peggy Sue's plight. She raised a commotion over Peggy Sue who was under the dining room table during the first part of the seizure. Becky followed Peggy Sue into the bedroom and sniffed her breath frantically every minute or so while I held her. What could Becky have been smelling? Oh how I wish these girls could talk.

Becky (Mom! Hey Mom! Come help! Peggy Sue is sick! Mom! Mom!)
Peggy Sue (Ohhhhh the world is spinning, and I can't walk and I'm scared and hold me Dad help me help me!)

Michael & Scotty Richardson
The Golden Girls
Becky: The Red Scourge of Squirrels, Feline Track Coach
Peggy Sue: Pixie, Lover of Every Creature, Fecal Gourmet

AND THEN THERE WERE THREE?

Had some old friends over for dinner Saturday night. Used the best linens.

Good china. Put on the dawg! When we started dinner, we had four nice linen napkins. Dinner ended, visiting started. Friends left late; we cleaned up the table. Now we only have three napkins. Hmmmmmm. Both the dogs were lying under the table at dinner. Did someone drop a napkin?

Hmmmm—could one of the girls have eaten it? Did it smell like pot roast?

We have only three viable options at this point: No. 1, our friends ripped us off for a napkin. No. 2, we lost it in one small room. No. 3, the dog ate it.

Hmmmm. You decide, see which you think is the most likely.

Soooooooo—it's poop patrol again. The fecal detective. Lawn taco surveyor. Boy, this is sure fun. So far five piles and *no* sign of the missing linen. But what an opportunity for puns and clichés!

"It'll all come out OK."

"Good things come to those who wait."

"All's well that ends well."

"Look for a sign, Tonto."

"I don't have a clue."

"Napkins happen."

"The proof is in the pooping." (sorry)

Becky (Why are you following me everywhere I squat? What are you looking for? Go away and let me go potty!)

Peggy Sue (You ate that napkin, didn't you? Sooner or later, we will have proof!)

Michael & Scotty Richardson
The Golden Girls
Becky: The Red Scourge of Squirrels, Feline Track Coach
Peggy Sue: Pixie, Lover of Every Creature, Fecal Gourmet

NICKNAMES?

So we're not the only weirdoes, eh?

Becky (aka Bailey's Teddy Bear): Fuzzbutt; Three-Meter Dog (so named because she's rarely farther than that from me); Becker-beast; Becker-head;
Becker-bee (from her habit of eating wasps); Garbage-gut; Killerbeast; Bouncing Becky (boing! boing!); Burr-butt; Goofy; Soopersquirrelgetter; etc.

Peggy Sue (aka Mt. Hood's Peggy Sue): Pooky; Woo-Woo-dog; Pigger; Miss
Piggy; Piggety-poo; Poopeater; Peggysuegetyourassinhere; Punkinhead; Airhead; Snaggletooth; Lovebugger; Sweetthing; Tacobreath; Sausagebuns; etc.

Becky (So now can I print the list of names I have for you?)
Peggy Sue (This is soooooooo embarrassing!)

Michael & Scotty Richardson
The Golden Girls
Becky: The Red Scourge of Squirrels, Feline Track Coach
Peggy Sue: Pixie, Lover of Every Creature, Fecal Gourmet

POOP BAGS? A MUST

My obedience instructor has a great line for offering a poo bag politely. She says to the plastic-challenged person: "Don't you hate it when you run out of bags on a walk? I've got an extra one you can have." Much more polite than "gonna pick that stuff up?"

Divine justice prevails—we have become the official poop-bag dispenser fillers for the local Park Service. In our basement, a box of about four hundred fancy little bags with wire bails is currently residing. We put these bags in a post-mounted dispenser a few at a time as the local hoodlums tend to toss them about. If I catch these varmints, I have suggestions for the authorities as to how to punish them. Use your imagination here. I am quick to mention the availability of these bags to the dog people we encounter on the trails. Just as long as they don't expect us to collect the bags when they are full, this should work.

Becky (Oh this is just sooooooo embarrassing. How low can you go?) Peggy Sue (Wow! Four hundred poop bags? Wow! How many? *Four hundred*? Makes me hungry just thinking about it!)

Michael & Scotty Richardson
The Golden Girls
Becky: The Red Scourge of Squirrels, Feline Track Coach
Peggy Sue: Pixie, Lover of Every Creature, Fecal Gourmet

DUMMIES? HUH?

Well, seems we have a tracking hound. Thought the girls might be bored with fetching tennis balls in the meadow, so decided to try a new game yesterday. I said to Michael: "Do you know where the dummies are?" Amazing response. Both dogs and Michael stood there and just looked at me. So embarrassing. So I exclaimed, "No, no, the *throwing* dummies!" Sheesh. Smart asses.

Now that issue was resolved, and the *throwing* dummies found, I grabbed a bottle of pheasant scent (how do they get that stuff in a squeeze bottle? I get this mental picture of someone squeezing a pheasant into a crumpled ball of feathers over a dish.) and applied it liberally to the dummy. Yeah, got some on myself too.

Down to the woods. Michael held the dogs while this dummy dragged the canvas dummy in a zigzag pattern through the meadow and hid it in some bushes. First, told Becky to "find the bird." She seemed clueless; flailed about aimlessly for a bit, so called her in and turned Peggy Sue aka "tracker" loose. Wow! She immediately jumped on the scent trail and found the scented dummy within a few seconds! Brought it to us and she was *sooooo* proud! Aced Becky!

Worked with Becky a bit more and she too returned the dummy, but she is far more random in her search. Does a big crossing pattern to find it. I think she would rather chase tennis balls. But Peggy Sue— anytime we were hiding/dragging the dummy, she would cry and kipe and whine with anticipation, and she never failed to find it even when I hid it in a tree!

She didn't want to quit the game and go home either. Are we on to something here? Any hot tips on training for tracking?

Becky (Why don't you just clobber that tennis ball for me—wanna chase it!)

Peggy Sue (Please, Dad, hide the dummy, please, will ya huh! Oh this is *so* much fun!)

Michael & Scotty Richardson
The Golden Girls
Becky: The Red Scourge of Squirrels, Feline Track Coach
Peggy Sue: Pixie, Lover of Every Creature, Fecal Gourmet

DOCTOR, DOCTOR!

Although I have been wiped out by both girls on frequent occasions generally involving tennis balls, sticks, etc., there's one particular incident neither Becky nor I are likely to forget.

While hiking up a steep trail in the Gifford Pinchot Wilderness in SW Washington State, Becky ran ahead of me up the hill and around a corner. Directly in front of me lying across the trail was a large (three feet diameter) log. Just as I threw my leg over the log at the critical point of balance, around the corner and down the hill at warp speed came Becky. As she knew the log was across the trail, she was already *in midair* coming directly at my skinny body, about chest high. That had to be the most incredible collision I have ever experienced. Most pro football players don't get hit that hard. And if they do, they weren't wearing a forty-pound backpack. Down on the ground we both went; me on my back with legs and arms kicking in the air like a beetle on its back. Tough to get up wearing a pack! Becky is lying next to me, a glazed look in her eyes. We both came to at about the same time. No permanent harm, but we both tend to be much more careful on the trails now. Man, but that's one hard-headed dog.

Becky (Who you calling hard-headed? You dang near broke my neck! Next time move off to the side of the trail!)
Peggy Sue (If you stoooopid field dogs would slow down a bit, the world would be safer for the rest of us! Slow down and live!)

Michael & Scotty Richardson
The Golden Girls
Becky: The Red Scourge of Squirrels, Feline Track Coach
Peggy Sue: Pixie, Lover of Every Creature, Fecal Gourmet

ONE UGLY COLOR

Well, the girls outdid themselves this time! While we were hunting mushrooms (Morels) in a semiarid area of Eastern Oregon, the girls managed to find an old cattle trough full of uh water. This thing hadn't been used for years, and the "water" was the consistency of split-pea soup. There must have been several inches of rust at the bottom of the trough. But did that stop the girls, in true golden fashion, from a quick dip? Of course not! When we stepped out of the brush and spotted them, Becky had completed her swim and had hopped out of the trough. But Peggy Sue was immersed except for her head in this reddish slime.

Now Becky is red to begin with. But Peggy Sue is (was) very blonde. You should have seen her when she flopped out of the trough; she was a bright orange color, except for her head. It stained her coat even a good bath didn't get much of it out. Sure looks funny! Anyone out there knows what to use to wash this orange color out, or should we relax and let time take care of it?

Peggy Sue (Way coool, duuuuude! I think I'm gonna get my ears pierced, maybe my nipples too! Hey, Mom, I'm into this punk thing. Help me fill out this application for Kurt Cobain's new church!)
Becky (You were bad enough with your "show dog" attitude. I'm not sure I'm gonna put up with this stuff. Turn down that boom box and take off those stupid sunglasses!)

Michael & Scotty Richardson
The Golden Girls
Becky: The Red Scourge of Squirrels, Feline Track Coach
Peggy Sue: Pixie, Lover of Every Creature, Fecal Gourmet

POPCORN, FOOTBALLS?

Are there actually golden owners out there who *don't* share popcorn with their dogs? Shame, shame. How selfish! :-) At our house, the ratio is about one kernel for me and three for each dog. And how about the fun of tossing a handful in the air to watch the fun? These critters are quick when they want to be! Doubt if feeding them popcorn is a problem for the dogs, been doing it for five years now.

If we tried to eat popcorn without sharing, our feet would be soaked in drool. Not to mention the psychotherapy fees made necessary by the guilt laid on us by these poor starving, underprivileged dogs.

'Nuff about popcorn. On to footballs. Found one for 50 cents at an estate sale today.

Brought it home to the girls. What a riot! Peggy Sue rolled on it, bumped it around the yard and spent an hour trying to figure out how to pack it around. Finally got it in her mouth, kind of by one end! Cute! So now the girls have a basketball, football, soccer ball, two softballs, several handballs, several baseballs, a dozen Frisbees, and roughly fifty (no kidding) tennis balls, sports fans! If you find a football for your dogs, buy it. I guarantee the entertainment value will more than pay the cost of the ball!

Peggy Sue (Man, this sucker is fun! It's got pointy ends and it doesn't bounce straight! Wheee!)
Becky (Yeah, well, it ain't gonna replace tennis balls.)

Michael & Scotty Richardson
The Golden Girls
Becky: The Red Scourge of Squirrels, Feline Track Coach
Peggy Sue: Pixie, Lover of Every Creature, Fecal Gourmet

STUPID GOLDENS?
DON'T THINK SO

Sorry, but I can't in good conscience allow our marvelous golden breed to be maligned. This missive is controversial at best, but I must point out that stupidity, and the varying degrees thereof, are a subjective matter.

Please bear with me and consider some of the following examples of what I consider stupid. Things your golden will *never* do, and conversely, some intelligent, exemplary things goldens *will* do. For instance, your golden will never:

Tie you to a stake on a six-foot chain and kick you when you complain. Grow tired of you, drive you to the country and dump you, alone and dejected to suffer a slow heartbroken death.

Nor will a golden grow tired of you and deposit you lonely and bewildered at the people pound.

Your golden will not use tobacco products, ruin its health, and litter the sidewalks with its butts.

Your golden will not become alcoholic or drug dependent and wreck its life and the lives of those around it. (No matter what some folks say about Bil-Jak!)

Your golden will never lead you on by saying "I love you" but not mean it.

Your golden will always respect you in the morning. There will be no "conditions" attached to your golden's love. A golden's love is always unconditional.

Your golden is unlikely to have a bad day and take it out on you.

Your golden will not go berserk or become anal if you burn breakfast.

Your golden will never pen a venomous flame letter on the Golden-L list and send it in the heat of the moment, only to suffer regret later.

Your golden will love all people, including children. Children *are* people. Your golden is wise and recognizes this. Children just haven't grown into their prejudices yet, as we adults (?) seem to.

If your golden suffers the "seven-year itch," it's probably just a flea and can be cured with a bath.

If your golden chooses to chase pussy, it will most likely be the neighbor's cat.

Your golden will not return home at 3:00 a.m. in a drunken stupor offering a batch of lame excuses after chasing the cat.

If your golden does choose to run off with the neighbor lady; your golden will only be gone as long as she has cookies to offer.

Your golden will never leave you for a younger, richer, or more comely person. Dogs see only the inner beauty. (And your cookies!)

Your golden does not care about social status. President or peasant, all the same. As it should be.

Your golden will not join the religious right and mandate how you should live your life. Your golden will not become a bigot. Your golden cares not for your sexual preferences or your choices in literature.

Your golden will not become involved in banning books it finds offensive from schools and libraries.

Neither will your golden become a flaming liberal and spend its welfare checks on 1960s records and books containing LSD-induced poetry.

Your golden will not shave its head and hang around airports passing out inane religious literature.

Your golden will never offer "the finger" to other motorists or shout obscenities at stupid people no matter how much they deserve it. Nor will your golden install huge really annoying speakers in its car and drive the streets late at night rattling plates off your walls.

Your golden will be as happy riding in an ancient VW van as in a Mercedes.

(Regardless of what Peggy Sue has said in the past!)

A golden desires no status symbols, no jewelry, no Rolex; just your love.

Your golden will not move to Montana with a diminished IQ and denounce its government, costing the taxpayers a fortune.

If your golden "dumps" on you, it's washable and will leave no permanent stains on your soul.

Your golden will remain steadfast, trusting, and loyal to you, even when you don't deserve it.

Your golden will suffer the bad times with you, and not walk away leaving you lonely and despondent. A soft, furry head in your lap can be very comforting at times.

'Nuff said. This has rambled enough. I hope I made my point.

Let the flames begin!

Becky (You blasted 'em this time, huh dad? But only stupid people would think goldens are stupid. How come they don't pick on cats? Now *cats* are a prime example of stupid!)

Peggy Sue (Well, perhaps some of you field dogs aren't as intelligent as we show stock. But stupid? No. Not stupid. Perhaps a bit slow. But hey, about these cats. If they're so dumb, how come you've never caught one?)

Michael & Scotty Richardson
The Golden Girls
Becky: The Red Scourge of Squirrels, Feline Track Coach

LAWN MOWIN' DAWG?

OK all, time to get shed of some of the arguing and serious stuff going on at the moment on this list! Neither of my dogs are ever very serious about anything. Except food, perhaps. Take a lesson from the dogs. Anybody else have a dog that follows you when you mow the lawn and *deliberately* drops her tennis ball directly in the path of the mower? Becky has discovered by placing the ball in such a manner, I have to stop and throw the danged thing. Takes me twice as long to mow the grass as it should. But it's more fun for both of us. Who was it that suggested goldens aren't very smart?

Becky (You can call me banal, single minded, even anal. I don't care what names you call. Just *keep on throwin' that tennis ball*! Lyrics by "Poop Doggy-Dog" for those of you not familiar with it!)
Peggy Sue (Oh, gawd. Red dog rap music. What next?)

Michael & Scotty Richardson
The Golden Girls
Becky: The Red Scourge of Squirrels, Feline Track Coach
Peggy Sue: Pixie, Lover of Every Creature, Fecal Gourmet

SPELING ERORS, ETC.

My dogs are soooo smart! Being the perfect goldens they are, they slept on a solution to all the furor created by the spelling and "grammer" posts here lately.

As this is an Olympic year, in keeping with international scoring rules Becky and The Pigger suggest the following.

Two new categories will be introduced to be used by the members of this list to judge the content and/or grammar of a post.

1. The *banalometer*. This should be used when judging the contents of a post. We can offer scores from 0-10 with 10 being perfectly banal. The girls had a hard time coming up with an award for this category, but they finally suggested a Jack Kevorkian certificate delivered in an old VW bus. Other suggestions are welcome.

2. The *analometer*. This category is scored using the same number system as above. However, this category should be judged on the degree of parsimonious poppycock, pompousness, sanctimoniousness, oversimplicity, arrogance, prejudice, etc. that a post contains. The girls had no trouble offering a suggestion for an award in this category. This award will be known as the *Peggy Sue award* and one turf-taco awarded for each point scored.

If we go to this system, we save bandwidth. Instead of a lengthy flame, just send a post with: banalometer, 9.5; analometer, 7.3, etc.

At the end of the year we can have a run off for the B.A. of the year! More Golden-L fun!

The girls pointed out that we should begin this system July 1, as a member of the list has just scored a perfect 10 in both categories (you know who you are! Congratulations! Your awards are in the mail!). I imagine/hope his computer is still smoldering from the flames. BTW, to the lawyer on the list—I hope I never need your services. But I know where I'm coming if I need a pointed letter written! :-)

Becky (I told you there was a way out of this bickering! Goldens hate bickering!)
Peggy Sue (OK, Becky, but I don't know why you couldn't use something for awards besides my berm burritos. I'm kinda stingy with those! But, this *is* a good cause!)

Michael & Scotty Richardson
The Golden Girls
Becky: The Red Scourge of Squirrels, Feline Track Coach
Peggy Sue: Pixie, Lover of Every Creature, Fecal Gourmet

PLUM NUTS, UPS?

UPS—Becky has developed a strange affinity for UPS (or FedEx, Airborne Express—picky she's not). Her first experience with UPS was rather alarming to me. I was mowing the lawn (safely, of course) around the back of the house. Becky *always* helps me mow, keeps my pace down by dropping one of her 3,234 (estimate may be low) damned tennis balls in front of the mower. All of a sudden—no Becky!

I shut down my turbocharged, stick-throwing, rock-hurling, poop-spreading (yeah, kidding here) Snapper and ran to the front yard. UPS truck at the curb, no driver, no Becky. Uh oh! Then I heard the giggling, roo-rooing, etc. She and the driver were on the floor of the truck merrily wrestling around, just having a great time. So much for the vicious killer dog image.

Unfortunately, she assumes *all* delivery persons, mailmen, garbage collectors, etc., come to visit her. Caused a bad scene with our no. 1 mailman. He's nervous about dogs, putting it mildly, and I try to keep Becky away from him, even though he doesn't have to get out of the truck to put the mail in the box. While no. 1 was on vacation, Becky formed a bond with his replacement. He would coax her over (not difficult!) to the truck; she would stand in the window to be petted. Yeah, you guessed it. The regular guy came back, she runs over and pokes her head in the truck, and he almost squirts out the other door. Ah well. I've been yelled at before. He called me something like "dirty pagalomer wrackafrack." His mouth was moving, no words coming out. Just foam. Snail mail flame job. He now realizes she is harmless, and all is well, the mail is getting delivered if Becky is out. She knows to leave him alone. He avoids eye contact with her.

The post about the dogs throwing their own ball and chasing it reminds me plum season is near. Our driveway is steep with a plum tree near the top. We came upon Becky dropping green plums at the top of the driveway in order to chase them as they flew down the hill in an elliptical orbit! Who said these dogs are dumb? As the plums ripen, she eats them instead of chasing them. Pits and all. So far everything has come out OK. ;-) ;-)

Becky (Plum season? The all-purpose fruit! The food with entertainment value! The original fruit with loops!)
Peggy Sue (Too much effort. I'll just lay here on my back in the sun while you act like an idiot. Bring me a ripe plum, would ya, Mom?)

Michael & Scotty Richardson
The Golden Girls
Becky: The Red Scourge of Squirrels, Feline Track Coach
Peggy Sue: Pixie, Lover of Every Creature, Fecal Gourmet

PEGGY SUE—KILLER DAWG?

Thought I'd seen it all. Been with these golden kids for about five years now. Always something new, eh? Took the girls to Vancouver Lake this morning. Thought a bit of water fun was in order. Took a tennis racket and a six-pack of balls. Started slamming balls one hundred yards or so into the lake; both girls really got into retrieving. After an hour or two of this and the 3,482 retrieves (possible exaggeration), both my arms and Peggy Sue began to tire. And Peggy Sue did a strange thing.

Mind you, if these dogs were people, Peggy Sue would wear white gloves, pink petticoats, and have high tea every day. Very much the lady. Becky, on the other hand, would wear plaid shirts, carry her keys clipped on her belt, and challenge men to arm-wrestling contests in beer joints.

Full-throttle dawg, so to speak.

On with the story. Peggy Sue stopped swimming out into the lake after the balls. Instead, she waited until Becky charged off after one and lurked in the shallows near me. As Becky returned the ball, Peggy Sue would crouch down and prepare to *charge!* When Becky was about twenty-five feet from shore—*feral dog* became all fangs, RRRRRRrrrrrr—bounce, bounce—POUNCE! She would dive on Becky's neck, causing Becky to drop the ball to defend herself. As soon as Becky dropped the ball, Peggy Sue would grab it and proudly return it to me, spitting it at my feet while

Becky frantically spun in circles out in the water looking for the ball.

Peggy Sue (Hahahahahah! Prepare to defend yourself, idjut red dawg! DROP that ball, I say! Here's the ball, dad! Ptui!)

Becky (Ooof! Ow! That hurts! What the—hey where's my ball?
Peggy Sue, I'm gonna kick your butt!)

Michael & Scotty Richardson
The Golden Girls
Becky: The Red Scourge of Squirrels, Feline Track Coach
Peggy Sue: Pixie, Lover of Every Creature, Fecal Gourmet

EATING CROW

I am choking on feathers. To those who have participated so far in the skin problem/color survey, please be advised my dogs have been tossed out of the results already.

The skin problems continued to worsen for the Pigger, and today, Becky began to develop red rash-like symptoms. Vet time. Both girls have a nasty bacterial infection and are now on antibiotics. Goodbye, paycheck.

Those of you living in the NW states affected by the terrible flooding please pay careful attention. According to our vet (who has been communicating with other area vets), these skin infections are of nearly epidemic proportion in this area and appear to be related to the flooding. Also the rate of giardia is more than double normal. Both my girls also suffered with that one earlier this year. I guess the message here is—there are some unusual problems related to the flooding to be aware of this spring. The symptoms Peggy Sue exhibited were similar to hot spots but began spreading rapidly after the second day we noticed them. Nothing seemed to help—not Gold Bond, Sulfodene, Calamine, Tar-sulfur baths, Benzoyl-peroxide baths, vinegar, rinse—tried 'em all. Nada. So be alert out there, this is one fast moving bacterial infection. Humorous note: Man brings sick dog in to vet's office. Dog has giardia. Man catches giardia from his dog. Man lands in the hospital. Man tries to provide his doctors with a stool sample. Man gets hernia from trying too hard. Just wasn't his day, I guess.

Becky (Well, it took me a week to come down with it. Red dogs are still tougher than blondies!)

Peggy Sue (You're probably the carrier! Typhoid Becky! Grrrrr! Itchscratchdig suck scratch)

Michael & Scotty Richardson
The Golden Girls
Becky: The Red Scourge of Squirrels, Feline Track Coach
Peggy Sue: Pixie, Lover of Every Creature, Fecal Gourmet

DOGS IN CARS?

Everyone who has posted to the list on this subject has a good point about the car becoming too warm for the dogs left untended. Our girls are never left in the car on a warm day. But I really must point out that there are other reasons for not leaving your dogs in an untended vehicle. For instance, we left the keys in the Hairmobile with Becky and Peggy Sue a while back. Mistake. Becky saw a cat. She stuffed that VW into gear and brought cat-chasing to a whole new level. Really hard to explain to the officer. Had to detail how I usually only let her drive while she's leashed, etc. Poor Peggy Sue along for the ride. Scared stiff. Becky isn't as good a driver as she is a retriever.

Becky (Boy, howdy! Did ya see the look on that cat's face?)
Peggy Sue (Dad won't let me drive because I can't reach the clutch. Wish they would buy something with an automatic.)

Michael & Scotty Richardson
The Golden Girls
Becky: The Red Scourge of Squirrels, Feline Track Coach
Peggy Sue: Pixie, Lover of Every Creature, Fecal Gourmet

HAIR COLOR RESULTS?

Looks like the last of the replies to the question of whether or not coat color (blondes vs. redheads) makes a difference with skin problems has trickled in.

I received information on forty different dogs. As for blonde dogs, I got six
who said yes, they have more problems with blondes. I got sixteen who said they didn't have any problems with their blonde dogs.
As for red dogs, three said they have skin problems, and fifteen said they have no skin problems. Not exactly a general consensus either direction. One side note: I received several *extremely defensive* replies from the owners of blonde dogs telling me that *no* way is there any correlation between skin problems and coat color. And no defensive replies from the owners of red dogs. Interesting.
Also several folks claim to have *never* had problems of any kind with their golden skin. Oh how I envy these people. I have to wonder though if these are the same people who think the hard drive on their computer will never crash?

Becky and the Pigger continue treatment. Peggy Sue is not doing well; she will begin a second round of antibiotics tomorrow. Becky has recovered and seems to be OK. We are watching them both closely, still bathing them every other day with benzoyl-peroxide. We tried the tea-tree oil that was supposed to clear up hot spots and keep the dogs from licking. Peggy Sue *loves* it. No accounting for her "tastes," is there? Had to quit using it. $10.00 for a small bottle. Cheaper to buy her caviar.
I chuckled at the posts about owning seven (or more) goldens and wondered how time-consuming and expensive this type of skin problem could become for these owners. Bathing two of them takes one and a half hours. Seven? But, I guess as with us and our two, the pleasure outweighs the pain!

Becky (Arrrrggghhhhh! Not another bath! I'm OK, I'm OK! Honest!)
Peggy Sue (Itch scratch suck bite chew snarfle slurp itch licklicklick)

Michael & Scotty Richardson
The Golden Girls
Becky: The Red Scourge of Squirrels, Feline Track Coach
Peggy Sue: Pixie, Lover of Every Creature, Fecal Gourmet

VOLCANIC ASH, UGH!

Caught the post from "down under" and thought I could at least commiserate with the volcanic ash problem. Having suffered the eruptions of Mt. St. Helens in 1980, I think we know what you are going through. At the time we had a Doberman who was used to doing daily seven-mile runs with me. We had one to three inches of ash *all* over the area (Portland, Oregon). The ash is about the consistency of fine sand, similar to what you find on the Caribbean beaches, except the ash is black. It gets into *everything*. We tried to stay inside until the worst of it settled, but our dog got nervous, as she was used to her exercise. Ate a hole in the wall-to-wall. I get nervous when I don't exercise too, but so far I haven't eaten any carpet. Anyway, I custom-fitted a surgical mask onto our dog (no easy task), put on my surgical mask, and went running. Must have looked really funny. The dog seemed to know the mask was necessary and didn't try to remove it until we got home. A quick rinse with the garden hose gets the worst of the ash off the dog's coat. After the city and the residents shoveled for a week or two, the worst of the ash was off the streets. It still ate up internal combustion engines, chainsaw blades, etc. for *a long time* after the eruptions. The Columbia River was closed to shipping for a while because the ash filled the channels. They had to be dredged. A real drag. Good luck down there, and "good on ya"! Volcanoes are a rather large problem.

Becky (A mask? Naomi ran with a mask? Cool! Can I have one?)
Peggy Sue (Try to fit one of those suckers on *my* schnozzle, and I'll eat your arm off right to the elbow! Grrrrr!)

Michael & Scotty Richardson
The Golden Girls
Becky: The Red Scourge of Squirrels, Feline Track Coach
Peggy Sue: Pixie, Lover of Every Creature, Fecal Gourmet

TICKS, DUMB BLONDES?

Becky and the Pigger have collected many ticks, despite our best efforts to keep the little beasties off them. Hiking areas in Washington and Oregon (Columbia Gorge in particular) are infested with ticks during spring and summer. Even when the dogs are sprayed with repellents, they pick up ticks. Gotten a few myself. Removing ticks is not an easy task once they are really buried. I've broken the heads off of lots of them. I don't care whose home remedy you use for tick removal. You can cover them with oil, burn them, nothing works every time. I've tried all the home remedies, believe me, nothing works except pulling them out with steady pressure while remaining patient.

We did purchase some "tick pliers" that help in the pulling process. They're little plastic pliers with a gap in the jaws to accommodate the tick's body. I break fewer ticks with these pliers than with tweezers unless the dog decides to jump or twitch at the wrong moment. We have never had an infection or an abscess from a broken off tick. Just a small bump usually, that the dogs body dissolves with time. Our girls are vaccinated against Lyme disease, and so far, so good. In a word, ticks, like AOL, suck.

Becky (I got one right in my, uhhh, rear end.)

Peggy Sue (They like my ears. The book says they like the hottest parts of the body. Guess your tick didn't read the book, eh Becky?)

Becky (Smart ass. Wanna hear a dumb-blonde joke, Peggy Sue? How did the blonde die while ice fishing? She was run over by the Zamboni!)

Peggy Sue (Very funny, you red idjut. It ain't easy being blonde.)

Michael & Scotty Richardson
The Golden Girls
Becky: The Red Scourge of Squirrels, Feline Track Coach
Peggy Sue: Pixie, Lover of Every Creature, Fecal Gourmet

END OF A-HAIRA?

I have mixed emotions as I write this—sadness, guilt, remorse. I have committed hairesy. The vehicle we have all come to know and love as the Hairmobile is no longer with us. Perhaps there are those of you on the list who won't consider this golden-related. It is. For the doubters among you, and for the record, when the VW was traded in yesterday after a short illness, it contained more golden hair than any of your kennels.

Pray for the detail shop that cleans it up. They will surely take a little of Becky and the Pigger home with them.

There were many golden miles traveled in that van, and each journey left a reminder. From the beach, sand. From the mountains, rocks, dirt, fir needles. From our friends Newfoundland, fleas. Ah fond memories. My wife's flea-bitten ankles. The dog hair that swirled about and lodged in my beard and on my clothes when a window was opened at speed. The night some poor soul broke into it and stole nothing, a result, we are certain, of choking on dog hair. Alas, after three major breakdowns inside of a week and scathing phone calls from a wife stranded in a bad part of town, the decision was made to part with the VW. Sigh.

Alas, the story becomes sadder still. We have joined the ranks of the nameless, faceless, masses. We have purchased the most blasé, benign, character-less, vehicle imaginable. A minivan. (GASP!) It will be difficult to display my wife's Grateful Dead stickers on this moving medium of mediocrity. Even the "Save the Whales" stickers will look out of place. I may have to shave my beard.

And out there somewhere tonight, alone and hirsute, the lonely Vanagon (Vanagone?) sits waiting for its next victim, er, owner. May they own two St. Bernards. And hiking boots. And a lifetime membership to AAA.

Becky (What's all the fuss? I like the new van! Except the glass is tinted and it screws up cow hunting. They all look green.)

Peggy Sue (*Where* is the Hairmobile? What have you done with it? Did you save all the woobies that were under the seat? I *want* my Hairmobile back!)

Michael & Scotty Richardson
The Golden Girls
Becky: The Red Scourge of Squirrels, Feline Track Coach
Peggy Sue: Pixie, Lover of Every Creature, Fecal Gourmet

CHAPTER TWO, THE EARNIE ERA

This was an exciting time. Also a little contentious. Our good friends bitch was about to give birth, and we had been asked to help with the whelping. There was a possibility we could have a male out of this litter. Michael, my lovely bride, was not so sure she wanted another dog. Me, of course, I sorely wanted a puppy. Stay tuned, strange things happened.

THE WAIT!
We are still in the wait mode on Chloe's puppers. Only Chloe knows for sure when the great event will happen. She looks ready, she's got bigger (and more) boobs than Pamela Anderson. The breeder called this a.m., all is about the same, but Chloe is now pacing and panting more. If the schedule holds true—Wednesday! This is exciting! Stay tuned to—pupperwatch '96!

Peggy Sue (I smell a *strange* dog on you—what are you up to? First you change cars—I hope you're not trading me in too!)

Becky (I smell a strange bitch on you too. Admit it—you've been unfaithful, haven't you?)

Michael & Scotty Richardson
The Golden Girls
Becky: The Red Scourge of Squirrels, Feline Track Coach
Peggy Sue: Pixie, Lover of Every Creature, Fecal Gourmet

PUPPY WATCH—OVER!

Gad, long day. And if the breeder, Michael, and I are tired, how about poor
Chloe? The final count was indeed nine. There are six boys and three girls. All are at least a pound except for one girl at fifteen ounces. We had a long wait on the final pup, over three hours. Seemed an eternity. Began to feel very sorry for Chloe, as she was beginning to look tired. Thankfully, she's in great shape. The last puppy was one of the largest males, and although a bit distressed, it came out squealing like anything. All in all—an exciting day. Our congratulations to The breeder. If these pups turn out anything like the rest of her dogs, they will be gorgeous animals with marvelous temperaments. We were proud to be a part of this whelping.

Becky (So now you go away *all* day and come home just reeking of other dogs. I suppose this means you don't love me anymore.)
Peggy Sue (Lighten up, you needy bitch! I smell a new playmate!)

Michael & Scotty Richardson
The Golden Girls
Becky: The Red Scourge of Squirrels, Feline Track Coach
Peggy Sue: Pixie, Lover of Every Creature, Fecal Gourmet

ROCKIN' DAWGS?

Do goldens in general have an ear for music and like to hop?

Can't speak for the whole breed. Becky likes live rock 'n roll. The radio won't do. Took Becky and The Pigger to a waterfront fair in Portland, Oregon, a while back. We were standing in the middle of a huge crowd, when this really loud band began to play. Becky started doing four-legged boing-boings in time to the music. She got really excited. Some of her boings were head high. Cracked up the crowd around us.
Also if we are leaving the house with the girls in it, we turn on the classical music station. The second they hear the classical music, they go and lie down. They know there is no hope of us giving in and letting them come along.

Becky (Gimmee a gittar, and put it in tune—we'll be rockin and rollin' soon!
Yeee—ha! Hot licks!)
Peggy Sue (I wanna go home. This sucks. Too many people, too much noise.
Humbug.)

Michael & Scotty Richardson
The Golden Girls
Becky: The Red Scourge of Squirrels, Feline Track Coach
Peggy Sue: Pixie, Lover of Every Creature, Fecal Gourmet

SYCHRONIZED WAGS

Chloe's puppies are now three days old, and today Michael and I observed a marvelous phenomenon. All nine one-pound bundles of joy lined up nursing, and *all* the little tails were wagging! So there you have it, listers. Goldens practically come out of the chute with wagging tails! Some of the little devils are *quite* vocal when they crawl off the wrong way in the whelping box and lose mom. Amazingly loud little squeals of dismay. Must be the females, huh? That's my sexist remark for the day. Seriously, these critters are *really cute*. Wonder how long Michael can hold out without falling in love with one of 'em. Time will tell.

Becky (I'm with Mom. I think there are enough dogs around here. Pay attention, Dad. If Momma ain't happy, ain't nobody happy.)
Peggy Sue (Hey you're not speaking for me. Maybe the pup would play with me like my cat friend Izzy did before the coyotes ate her. I'd like another playmate. And I promise not to teach him the fine art of poop-eating. 'Cause it makes Mom and Dad really anal!)

Michael & Scotty Richardson
The Golden Girls
Becky: The Red Scourge of Squirrels, Feline Track Coach
Peggy Sue: Pixie, Lover of Every Creature, Fecal Gourmet

THE PUPPIES!

One week and one day, and the puppers and Chloe are doing fine! Michael has been doing puppy-sitting for the last week along with the breeder's mom and dad. The pups are growing by leaps and bounds. Most have gained about three-fourths of their original body weight. We will now begin checking on them about every two hours or so, instead of a constant vigil and see how that works out. We live about a mile from the breeder, so I pumped up the tires on Michael's mountain bike. Let's see—every two hours, four or five trips a day—good for about ten miles of exercise for Michael! Stay tuned for more updates, so far, so good!

Becky (I still smell strange going on here. Made me lose my concentration while fetching. Ran into the fence, all your fault. My head hurts.)

Peggy Sue (Nice try, dumb excuse. I always said you field dogs weren't too smart. Always telling dumb-blonde jokes. Now who's the dummy?)

Michael & Scotty Richardson
The Golden Girls
Becky: The Red Scourge of Squirrels, Feline Track Coach
Peggy Sue: Pixie, Lover of Every Creature, Fecal Gourmet

BEWARE THE FENCE

A normal day at the Richardsons. Becky, The Pigger, and I went for a five-mile jaunt. Took the tennis racket, whacked some balls in the meadow for the girls. A bit warm for the girls, perhaps eighty degrees or so, so they tired quickly. Home we go! While they're tired, trim the toenails. Use the electric shears, trim the feet. This always wires 'em. Becky bounces up to me with a tennis ball. I am standing on the outside of our chain-link fence, the gate is open. I throw the ball for her. She doesn't bother with the gate, runs lickety-brindle right into the chain link fence, full-tilt boogie—missed the gate by a good four feet. *Wham!* She dribbles off the fence, staggers through the gate, and gets the ball. Then she glares at me as if to say "when did you move that fence?" Guess she's OK, she's "helping" Michael in the kitchen. Gotta love 'em. Laugh a minute!

Becky (Oooooooo! That smarts! Where *did* that fence come from?)
Peggy Sue (If it smarts, try rubbing some on your head, you red idjut. Maybe now is the time for a dumb redhead joke, eh?)

Michael & Scotty Richardson
The Golden Girls
Becky: The Red Scourge of Squirrels, Feline Track Coach
Peggy Sue: Pixie, Lover of Every Creature, Fecal Gourmet

REMOVING SAP? A SNAP

Any good ideas on how to get tree sap off my GR's? All three have gotten small spots on their backs from a tree in our yard. Maybe one of the field crowd have a cure all for this type of thing.

Any and all suggestions welcome.

Thanks!

We use *real* butter. The enzymes (or something) in *real* butter work wonders on tree sap. Becky and The Pigger have probably gone through twenty pounds of butter so far. Plus, of course, they like to lick it off. I tried licking it off them, but it increased my cholesterol. (Just kidding!) Seriously, only genuine butter does the trick, not margarine or any other butter substitute. Try it, it works! Rub it in well, Michael reminds me— and wait a little bit, five minutes or so. The sap will wipe, comb, or lick right out. Also, and for obvious reasons, I *do not* recommend this—in a pinch, WD-40 will cut tree sap.

Becky (Use the butter, Dad! Mmmmmmmmmmm!)
Peggy Sue (Yeah, just call me butterball! Think I'll find some more pitch to roll in!)

Michael & Scotty Richardson
The Golden Girls
Becky: The Red Scourge of Squirrels, Feline Track Coach
Peggy Sue: Pixie, Lover of Every Creature, Fecal Gourmet

A THORNY SUBJECT

Becky, even as I type, is out picking blackberries. Understand that this is no mean feat. We are talking those little wild berries on bushes with thorns all over them. But she's out there, tail going like mad, pulling them off and scarfing them down.

Both our goldens (as was our departed Doberman) are "berry pickers." The trail below our home is thick with Himalayan blackberries right now. We humans consider these danged vines a scourge. I've fought them *all my life,* but the dogs love the berries this time of year. They will "pucker" their lips and pull the berries off the vines very carefully to avoid the thorns. Of course, the berries I hand-feed them are much tastier than the ones they pick. Even better than the blackberries are the wild mountain huckleberries just beginning to ripen along the trails in our mountains this time of the year. There are four different species, and the girls have learned that the reddish ones are tart and not nearly as tasty as the fat black ones. Perhaps it is smell rather than color, but they *do* know the difference. Probably the only dogs I know who gain weight on long hikes.

Peggy Sue (Picking these berries myself is beneath my dignity. However, if you hand feed me, perhaps I can be coerced into eating a few.)
Becky (Outa my way, lard-butt. I would kill for fresh berries! MMMMM these are really sweet. Every once in a while I get a sour one. Makes my face pucker up. Ptui! There's a sour one now!)

Michael & Scotty Richardson
The Golden Girls
Becky: The Red Scourge of Squirrels, Feline Track Coach
Peggy Sue: Pixie, Lover of Every Creature, Fecal Gourmet

LOBBY FOR DOGBERT?

The lobbying continues here for the new puppy. I am still getting a certain amount of resistance from my wife. Today though, their little eyes are open, and are they ever cute! Michael cuddled a few of them. I think her resistance is lowering. Took her to dinner the other night, wined, dined, picked the critical moment to pop the question, and she (almost) said yes. Almost had her. So close. But the next day, same story. Goes like this:

Scotty: Geez, aren't the little guys cute? And wouldn't a third dog, a cute little boy, make a nice addition to our household?
Michael: Yeah, I admit they are cute. But who's gonna train him? Me! While you work. And feed him? And take him out to potty? And keep Becky *from killing him for the first few weeks? Me, that's who!*
Scotty: Well, sure, perhaps he might cause a bit of inconvenience at the beginning, but think of the laughter he's sure to bring, and the love, etc.
Michael: Yeah, and the chewed up shoes, peed on rugs, the whining at night, and more vet bills.
Scotty: Minor items, minor items. Little Dogbert is sure to capture your heart!
Michael: Probably. We'll see. Humph.

The debate continues. The breeder of course, is on my side and has explained to Michael what a wonderful bond forms with a dog when you have been there from the whelping. Makes sense, the pups all know Michael's smell from birth and have smelled her and now are seeing her practically every day.

So stay tuned as the critical period begins! The pups will be ready to take home in a few weeks! Will we have a third dog? Wait and see!

Becky (If you bring that little fur ball in here, I'll kick his butt!)
Peggy Sue (Lighten up, red bitch! The more, the merrier!)

Michael & Scotty Richardson
The Golden Girls
Becky: The Red Scourge of Squirrels, Feline Track Coach
Peggy Sue: Pixie, Lover of Every Creature, Fecal Gourmet

BEGGING FOR THE
PUPPY, NAMES, ETC.

So stay tuned as the critical period begins! The pups will be ready to take home in a few weeks! Will we have a third dog? Wait and see!

Heh, heh, heh! No question in *my* mind. Just wait 'til they hit six to seven weeks.
Nobody can resist them then.

But you're not really going to name him Dogbert, are you?

Are you?

Hmmmmm. Got a private post tonight suggesting Buddy. Short for Buddy
Holly—as in Peggy Sue—y'know? I guess we're open for suggestions.
However, if you read Dilbert (who doesn't) you just have to appreciate Dogbert's attitude. Anybody wanting to be supreme ruler of the universe can't be all bad. OK, so I'm weird. I do know we won't name him Bill, Bob, or Newt. Or Sue.

Becky (Hey don't I get to vote on this? I'll name the little sucker MUD! Right after I adjust his attitude for him—)
Peggy Sue (Buddy Holly does have a nice ring to it, doesn't it? Hey, Mom, if we name him Buddy can we bring him home?)

Michael & Scotty Richardson
The Golden Girls
Becky: The Red Scourge of Squirrels, Feline Track Coach
Peggy Sue: Pixie, Lover of Every Creature, Fecal Gourmet

MACHO GOLDENS?

After a full afternoon of batting tennis balls into the Columbia River for my girls, we stopped at a roadside stand to buy some fresh corn. Two soggy goldens in the back of the truck (yes, inside a canopy!). Everything was cool until two *really* old people (definition: older than us) pulled in next to us with two Chihuahuas about the size of rats in their car. These itty-bitty dogs had an attitude. Started lunging at the windows of the car, shrieking at Becky and The Pigger. Who of course, then barked in return. Sounded terrible! The lady in the store was alarmed at the terrible deep barking emanating from our truck. I told her: "Hey they're just goldens."

"Goldens?" she said. "I *just love* goldens!" So out to the truck, down with the tailgate, while this lady loves the two very wet girls. It takes a real dog lover to cuddle two soaked, sandy goldens. All the while, the rat-dogs continued with their hysterics. But

Becky and The Pigger were far more interested in the lovin' than rat-dogs hysterics. Priorities, I guess.

Becky (Hey I can kick those dust-mop dogs butts later, right now I've got a hot one on the hook! Gimmee some lovin'!)

Peggy Sue (Pet me! Pet meeeeeee! Dad, could you shut those idiot midget dogs up? They're getting on my nerves!)

Michael & Scotty Richardson
The Golden Girls
Becky: The Red Scourge of Squirrels, Feline Track Coach
Peggy Sue: Pixie, Lover of Every Creature, Fecal Gourmet

THE LOBBYING WORKED!

Yessssssss! Michael has (finally) agreed to let us have a puppy! Wow, what an arduous sales job this has been. Started in December—took the last eight months to get her to say yes.

I wined her, dined her. No sale. I whined, I sniveled. Nope. I promised to pick up my clothes. Nah. I promised to lower the toilet seat. She liked that one, but it wasn't enough. I bought her a car. Nice, but still no sale. Got her personalized license plates. "TREHUGR" for those of you who are curious. (The chainsaw wielding husband better not wield his chainsaw around this house.) But I digress. What finally turned the trick, with a little help from the pups who now run across the whelping box, tails wagging to greet us was this—I agreed to get a couple of chairs reupholstered for her. Yeah, go figure. Also she gets to name the pup. There will be no Dogbert. No Buddy. No Jughead. His name is Earnie. Yes, I spelled it right. Michael says she earned this pup—what with all the mothering she has been doing with the litter. (She loves it!) So she suggested Earnie. OK by me; all the Ernies I know are nice guys. Not a politician in the bunch. Please accept my gratitude, for those of you who wrote in my behalf on this issue, and there were many of you! Poor Michael, worldwide pressure! Now if I can just convince Becky this is all OK when we bring Earnie home?

Becky *(What? You are bringing what home? You had better not bring a puppy into this house unless he's edible!* ARGGGGHHHHHHHHH!)
Peggy Sue (Will Earnie play with me? I can protect him from the red bitch too! RRRRRRRRR!)

Michael & Scotty Richardson
The Golden Girls
Becky: The Red Scourge of Squirrels, Feline Track Coach
Peggy Sue: Pixie, Lover of Every Creature, Fecal Gourmet

CHAPTER TWO?

Around this time things began to be –interesting. Earnie, the new puppy so named because we "earned" him, begins to take a large chunk of our lives. One forgets over the years how much work a puppy can be. Earnie was a hoot, and a rascal. He was nicknamed "The Great White Humper" for reasons that will become obvious. A lot of big stuffed toys went to the "Great Dumpster in the Sky," even though the boy was neutered. Problem was, he never seemed to know that?

GOLDEN WOOBIE KILLERS?

Ah! So now I realize there are good and evil woobies! That explains a lot. I also have been enlightened as to why although my girls *never* (almost) destroy their woobies, they occasionally remove the eyes from them. Blind evil woobies are unable to see to attack. I should have thought of that. Becky likes to deprive the woobies of their sense of smell as well and removes the button noses. Problem with some of this is that she swallows the eyes, etc. Almost lost it one evening when I saw a pile of poop staring at me from the grass. No wonder the dogs wouldn't use that part of the yard until I cleaned it up.

Becky (Well, I didn't think you realized the danger we were all in. So I blinded the little monsters! And swallowed the eyes so they couldn't see!)
Peggy Sue (Boy, that pile of poop with the eye in it almost scared me witless. I never eat a turf-taco that stares at me.)

Michael & Scotty Richardson
The Golden Girls
Becky: The Red Scourge of Squirrels, Feline Track Coach
Peggy Sue: Pixie, Lover of Every Creature, Fecal Gourmet

LANGUAGE BARRIER?

Got to our favorite beach today to find two cars parked above it. It's a small area, soft sand, perfect for the dogs. Not wanting to screw with someone else's solitude, I walked down to the beach to see how occupied it was before turning the wild dogs (they saw water) loose. Turned out there were only two folks there—both elderly Oriental gentlemen, fishing for sturgeon. I asked if it was OK with them if I worked my dogs on the beach.

They both grinned widely and said, "Yes, yes!" I asked them if they had caught any fish. "Yes, yes!" Were they having a nice day? "Yes, yes!" At about this point, I realized they had no clue what I was saying as they spoke no English. I could have asked if they minded me driving one hundred head of cattle through there. To hell with it, I went and got the girls out of the truck. As they thundered past the two fishermen, Becky and The Pigger discovered the fish-bait. Rotten herring, yum, yum! The two fishermen both jumped up and shouted, "No, no!" So guess they knew a little more English than we thought. What really threw them was what the devil my tennis racket was for. After swatting a couple of balls out to midstream, they nodded at each other and went back to fishing. Just another crazy American.

Becky (Those guys were great! They always say yes!)
Pigger (Yeah, except when we found the bait. Boy, that smelled really delicious too.)

Michael & Scotty Richardson
The Golden Girls
Becky: The Red Scourge of Squirrels, Feline Track Coach
Peggy Sue: Pixie, Lover of Every Creature, Fecal Gourmet

HEARTBREAKERS

Chloe's litter of nine is now just over a month old. They are absolutely drop-dead cute. They have even won the heart of my bride, Michael, who is now looking forward (I think) to the arrival of little Earnie. Please, God, don't let Earnie be "The Pup From Hell" as Michael will remind me this was my idea forever. At least, when you're as old as we are, forever may not be as long as it is for some of you! (VBG) Today, the pups went outside for the first time. Mixed response. Some were very curious, others just *wanted back in!* One little girl threw back her head, made her mouth into a perfect "O" and howled! Looked like a miniature White Fang! OWWWWooooooooo! Cracked us up! The whelping box was moved into a spare room and the bottom covered with wood shavings. The new texture was fascinating to the little critters, and they took big mouthfuls of the stuff to sample it. Looked real funny, wood chips on their chins like little beards. They are eating real food like little pigs, with some of them climbing right into the food bowl. What a mess! But the sight of nine little butts sticking up in the air around that food bowl is a Kodak moment, for sure.

Peggy Sue (I sure hope Earnie doesn't out-cute me, and that he's half the fun to play with that my cat was.)

Becky (What makes you think he's going to live long enough to play with you? Let me at 'im!)

Michael & Scotty Richardson
The Golden Girls
Becky: The Red Scourge of Squirrels, Feline Track Coach
Peggy Sue: Pixie, Lover of Every Creature, Fecal Gourmet

PET STORE WOOBIES

Becky and The Pigger have been following this thread. They wish to make the following observation: The problem with the evil woobies is where they come from. Evil woobies can only be found at pet stores. That's where they hang around and pick up bad habits. Usually from too much exposure to cats or something. Or teenagers, you know ;-)! They point out that between the two of them, they have a herd of woobies numbering (seriously) about forty. Out of this number, only one, a Chewman ordered from a pet store, has ever lost its life in our home. He was bad to the bone. It was a slow death too. One seam at a time. The remainder of the woobies came from garage sales and rummage sales, etc. These woobies started their lives as human baby toys and didn't pick up bad habits from cats, etc. Also, they add, the Chewman cost $7.00, and the most expensive of the remaining woobies was around $0.50 or so. Becky does admit to blinding a few; you probably recall the post about where woobie eyes and noses eventually end up.

Becky (I remember that Chewman. A regular polyester Chester. Not only did he come from a pet store, he was from back east somewhere. Probably picked up his bad habits in the Chicago 'burbs.)
Peggy Sue (Oh yeah. He was a rough one. We had to work together to off that sucker. Now he just lies all flat in the bottom of the toy box. We showed him—)

Michael & Scotty Richardson
The Golden Girls
Becky: The Red Scourge of Squirrels, Feline Track Coach
Peggy Sue: Pixie, Lover of Every Creature, Fecal Gourmet

POOR MAN'S PEACHES?

Becky insists upon eating a fresh pear from our tree every time "we" mow the lawn together. She ate all the low ones she could reach. Now she stands under the tree looking up at the pears soulfully until I give in and pick her one.

About the dog that eats slugs—check to see if the dog has any French ancestors. Anyway, here in the great NW we refer to banana slugs as "poor man's peaches." This may just change the way you look at a jar of canned peaches for the rest of your life. :-(

Becky (I eat just about anything—but *not* slugs. Oh YUCK!)
Peggy Sue (Hey, I bet this means you won't be complaining about my little scatological difficulty anymore, eh? Poop is one thing—but slugs? Now *that's* disgusting!)

Michael & Scotty Richardson
The Golden Girls
Becky: The Red Scourge of Squirrels, Feline Track Coach
Peggy Sue: Pixie, Lover of Every Creature, Fecal Gourmet

SMELLY SUBJECT

Hi everyone.

This topic is a real stinker. Pardon the pun. I too have a golden that used to have this problem, and one that is beginning to make me wonder if I don't need to have her flushed out. Read on . . . .

Becky suffered from this problem (actually, we suffered together) when we first brought her home. She was a little over a year old at the time. After paying the vet $15.00 to "express" (interesting terminology) her anal glands several times, I bought a gross (gross applies here) of rubber gloves and learned the ol' finger wave myself. It's not a difficult maneuver. Of course, Becky's opinion may not be the same as mine, and I notice she leaves the room if she spots a rubber glove. I am (very) happy to say that in the last year (she's six) the problem has all but disappeared. Hallelujah.

Becky (Amen.)
Peggy Sue (Whatever is the old pervert up to now, Becky?)

Michael & Scotty Richardson
The Golden Girls
Becky: The Red Scourge of Squirrels, Feline Track Coach
Peggy Sue: Pixie, Lover of Every Creature, Fecal Gourmet

THE END?

Once again, sad to say, I have been ridiculed by a person on this list. Usually, this is a result (as in this case) of the person doing the ridiculing being uninformed, uneducated, or just possibly, a general know-it-all. On the subject of the back half of our dogs. Pay attention.

The back half is *just as important*, yea, even *more* so, than the front half. I will use an old fable to illustrate my case. This is the story of the terrible "hippogater," meanest animal on earth. It has the front half of a hippopotamus on one end. And the front half of an alligator on the other end. So you ask, if it's got a hippo head on one end and an alligator head on the other end, how does it, er, poop? Well, it doesn't. And that's what makes it so mean.

It's very important that what goes in the front, comes out the back. If it doesn't, the results can be devastating. I work for a guy who hasn't had a BM in thirty-seven years. But that's another story. We all value our goldens' temperament. Do you think they would be so sweet if they were constipated all the time? Of course not! Hey look at some famous folks—Bob Dole, now there's a guy packing a load. Newt—wow! Look at their eyes. Even a person with little knowledge of *the back half* can see there's a problem here. So next time you make fun of somebody just because they specialize in *the back half,* I suggest you look in the bathroom mirror and think about what I just wrote. And then reach for the Ex-lax. Are you part of the problem or the solution? Hey it's a dirty job, but someone has to do it.

Becky (Is this what they mean by "the better half" when Mom and Dad talk about each other?)

Peggy Sue (Could be. But why does Mom compare Dad to the back half of a horse? I fail to see the resemblance?)

Michael & Scotty Richardson
The Golden Girls
Becky: The Red Scourge of Squirrels, Feline Track Coach
Peggy Sue: Pixie, Lover of Every Creature, Fecal Gourmet

SLIPPERY GOLDENS?

I was amused at the posting about the golden using the playground slide. Don't all goldens do that? I have pictures of Becky coming down a playground slide. I was in a wacky mood (getting more frequent since I made the over-the-hill gang) and decided to slide down the playground slide. Up the ladder I go! Halfway down, Michael says, "Look at Becky!"

She followed me up the ladder, and down the slide she came. We repeated this several times after going home for the camera. Pretty funny! She has also made it most of the way up a twenty-foot extension ladder trying to help me work on the roof. I had to help her down from this venture. While swimming in the Washougal River a couple of years ago, I did a cannonball off a ten-foot-high rock ledge—looked up as I hit the water—here comes the Red Dog!

Peggy Sue, however, views things like playground equipment as dangerous.

Killer slides, swings, etc. Go figure? So far, I haven't found any place I would go where Becky won't. Including the bathroom. I have learned to close the door. Some things are best done alone.

Becky (I'm a slip-slidin' fool! Huh. Dad?)
Peggy Sue (Well, Becky, you're half-right!)
Becky (OK, smart ass, I'm gonna tell a dumb-blonde joke just for that. Here goes—What do you call fifteen blondes in a circle? A dope ring! Hahahahah!)
Peggy Sue (Grooaaannn!)

Michael & Scotty Richardson
The Golden Girls
Becky: The Red Scourge of Squirrels, Feline Track Coach
Peggy Sue: Pixie, Lover of Every Creature, Fecal Gourmet

THE *BIG* DECISION!

The time has come. It will be seven weeks tomorrow. The puppies are ready for their new homes. And we must choose between six adorable males to find our

Earnie. Arrrrggghhhhh! How do we do this? I want them *all*. After taking care of them on a daily basis since their birth, we have naturally fallen in love with all of them. Choosing a wife was easy. Is she beautiful? Intelligent? Does she have money? A boat? Does she like to fish and hunt? Ride bicycles? Will she listen when you talk to her? Check her teeth, make sure she's telling the truth about her age. All checks out? Marry her, live happily forever after.

But this puppy choice. They are all beautiful. They all listen when I talk to them. Great teeth. I know their ages. Tough choice. And whichever puppy we choose will leave us feeling guilty about the ones who were sitting next to me, leaning on my leg saying in puppy language—"Take me home! I think I love you!" Oh the guilt!

Seriously, there are three we have narrowed the choice down to. Probably actually two. One is quiet, very cuddly, tends to wait until the others are over their initial excitement when we see them to come over for his loving. A calm puppy. Relaxed. Doesn't stiffen up when picked up and turned over, etc. Trusting. Unafraid of anything. The other puppy is similar, except he *cannot get enough* of us. Always the first to get to us, wants constant attention. We are even more important than his food.

Now the important part. Puppy no. 1 is Michael's favorite. Puppy no. 2 is my favorite. But neither is an overwhelming favorite. My gut feeling is to go with Michael's favorite so when he eats the antique couch, she won't be able to say: "I told you we should have gotten my favorite."

Help! What to do? Crunch time is here! By this time tomorrow, it will be done!

Becky (It'll be done all right. If I can just get to him to make sandwich spread!)
Peggy Sue (Can I train him to eat poop and be hard of listening?)

Michael & Scotty Richardson
The Golden Girls
Becky: The Red Scourge of Squirrels, Feline Track Coach
Peggy Sue: Pixie, Lover of Every Creature, Fecal Gourmet

DECISION—MADE!

There is a God. We have a *new* golden retriever brother for our girls! By the time we arrived at the breeder's house tonight the decision had been made *for* us. The breeder had made the decision! As luck would have it, we ended up with the no. 1 pick male, as there is no show home for him. We agreed to not neuter the pup until he is twelve to fifteen months old just in case he turns out to be *the* show boy. This really lifted a huge weight off of Michael and I. Now neither of us is to blame if Earnie eats the couch!

The pups we had arbitrarily chosen as *our* no. 1 and no. 2 picks turned out to be graded the no. 2 and no. 3 males. The puppy who has become Earnie would have been our third choice. However, remember, we don't know squat about conformation, etc. We are primarily interested in personality. This pup has personality plus! Perfect!

The breeder gets to watch Earnie to see how he develops, and we get the *pick* of the boys! What could be better than that? *He is really cute!* Sorry, just needed to shout that. Earnie is *all* cuddles, loves to be held. No fear! Very calm, cool, collected. We are very happy, and tomorrow we bring him home to meet the girls. I am reasonably certain they will be *less than thrilled*. Oh well, can't please everybody! Thanks for all your support, we received an unbelievable number of posts and opinions, and we learned *a lot*. I love this list! Thank you, thank you, thank you!

Becky (Hey, Pigger, if you help me put Earnie in the Cuisinart, we'll make puree out of him!)

Peggy Sue (Think we can get the lid on? Here. I'll sit on it.)

Michael & Scotty Richardson
The Golden Girls
Becky: The Red Scourge of Squirrels, Feline Track Coach
Peggy Sue: Pixie, Lover of Every Creature, Fecal Gourmet

PUPPIES ARE LIKE SURGERY?

Arrrggghhh. Getting a new puppy after five years of no puppies is a *lot* like having surgery. You know, the doctor says "no sweat, we'll just cut right here and here and take this out and sew this up. No big deal." Sounds reasonable. But after the surgery, you wake up and remember why you swore you'd never have surgery again. With time, you forget the pain.

Ahhh, yesss! We had forgotten some of the benefits of a new pup. The really gorgeous yellow contrast of the puppy pee on the white linoleum floor. The chewed fringes of the couch. The killer attacks with needle sharp teeth on your bare toes. The midnight, 2:00 a.m., 4:00 a.m., and 6:00 a.m. whining and kiping from the crate in our bedroom. Yes, he spent his first night in our room with us and the girls. He will spend *all* his nights in our bedroom, no matter how much sleep we lose. He *is* family now. This is great!

Becky has mellowed in twenty-four hours to the point where her growls are less menacing. She still refuses to drink from the water dish if Earnie has used it. Peggy Sue is no problem, some initial snarling, sneering, etc. Today, she allows him to step on her face and lie next to her. She's really a sweetheart.

Earnie has true golden temperament. He shows interest in everything, but no fear. He got his first bath in the kitchen sink today; he really enjoyed it. He knows Becky is a *real bitch* and avoids her unless I am in the room. He already thinks I'm alpha. Hope he doesn't tell Michael. Earnie seems already to have bonded with us, particularly Michael. Probably astute enough at seven weeks to know she's the soft touch around here.

I think this is going to work—if we can just mellow Becky out. Any suggestions on how to do this would be really appreciated! She'd better get used to Earnie—he's already family.

Becky (Peggy Sue, run out to the woodshed and bring me the axe, will ya?)
Peggy Sue (I know you're the boss, you red bitch. But I think I'm beginning to like him. I have a *brother!* Get your own axe.)

Michael & Scotty Richardson
The Golden Girls
Becky: The Red Scourge of Squirrels, Feline Track Coach
Peggy Sue: Pixie, Lover of Every Creature, Fecal Gourmet

A BABY SEX MANIAC?

Earnie is now two days short of eight weeks. He's doing really well here at home with potty training—one accident in two days. He goes to the door already when he needs out. The trick is being there in a hurry as he can't hold it very long. No messes at all in the kennels. That's the good news. Read on—

The night before last after bringing him in from potty we had to dry him with a towel as it was raining cats and dogs. When we put him on the floor, he proceeded to "hump" the towel. Last night, he graduated to humping the larger woobies. In particular, "big bear," a teddy twice his size. Quite a sight—an eight-week-old pup, chewy in his mouth, blithely humping away at a teddy twice his size. I checked the teddy—can't tell if it's a boy or a girl. Hmmm. Is this just puppy dominance? Should we discourage this behavior? Will it go away with age?

Becky (I told you we should have barbecued him.)
Peggy Sue (If he doesn't leave me alone when I'm trying to go potty, I may provide the sauce.)
Earnie (Hey, bear, how 'bout a cigarette?)

Michael & Scotty Richardson
The Golden Girls
Becky: The Red Scourge of Squirrels, Feline Track Coach
Peggy Sue: Pixie, Lover of Every Creature, Fecal Gourmet
Earnie: aka White Shark, Lawn Thatcher

THE TEDDY SNATCH?

Sorry, just can't work up my blood pressure about this Japan stuff. Forgive me for getting off the track. But I find this amusing—Earnie at eight weeks has perfected what will always be known in this house as the "Teddy snatch." Goes like this: Becky's packing a Teddy bear loosely in her mouth. She sits in front of one of us, bear in mouth, waiting to be petted. Earnie figured out that by rocketing under her chin at *warp 9* and grabbing the bear he's gone before she can react. However, today when he pulled that little stunt at breakfast, Becky let out a roar that would have stopped a charging rhino. It also stopped Earnie who dropped the bear and went into a submissive position. Dunno what Becky said, but I've *got* to learn that command!

Becky (DROP that bear, you pesty little sucker, before I make an unstuffed woobie out of you!)
Peggy Sue (Hee hee hee. Sure glad there's another blonde in the house. Hey, Becky, who's the dummy now? GO, EARNIE!)

Michael & Scotty Richardson
The Golden Gang
Becky: The Red Scourge of Squirrels, Feline Track Coach
Peggy Sue: Pixie, Lover of Every Creature, Fecal Gourmet
Earnie: aka Small White Shark, Grass Gobbler, Teddy Snatcher

THE GREAT WHITE RAT?

Sounds silly, but we've decided it'll be a great day when Earnie grows too large to get under the furniture. He's discovered that old people have a really difficult time following him under the couches, futons, chairs, etc. in our home. If he gets under one end of the futon and you try to grab him, he shoots the length of it thumping his head on each cross-brace (thump-thump-thump-thump) as he runs. He looks for all the world like a large white rat. When he squirts out from under the end of the futon, Pigger is waiting to dive on him. Great game, if you're a dog. Both Michael and I are suffering from hyperextended arms and sore knees. Becky and The Pigger love it though. They join us on the floor, butts in the air, noses under the couch, as if to say, "I found him!" If this keeps up, as we're sure it will, Michael and I will be more flexible than a yoga master. Pray for us. Aren't puppies fun? :-(

Becky (Dang! I hate it when that pestilent pip squeak pops out from under the furniture at me! C'mere Earnie, let me show you this barbecue. That's it, closer, closer—hehhehheh!)
Peggy Sue (Where's Earnie? Huh? Where is that squirt? Hey this is a great game!)
Earnie (Fast as fast can be—you'll never catch meeeee! Thumpthumppow myheadowow)

Michael & Scotty Richardson
The Golden Gang
Becky: The Red Scourge of Squirrels, Feline Track Coach
Peggy Sue: Pixie, Lover of Every Creature, Fecal Gourmet
Earnie: aka Small White Shark, Grass Gobbler, Teddy Snatcher

THE DREADED URPA-GURKAS?

Peggy Sue is reading this, and she likes the idea. However, I'm so danged depressed from the tone of the list lately I doubt I can even get into a poop thread. Well, perhaps, if I'm prompted a bit.

This has prompted me to make a confession. My Harvey's first impression of the fishy smelling beach sand was to *eat* it. I tried my best to keep things to a minimum. However, the next day there it was—a "section" that was *all sand, yes, all sand!* I remarked to George (husband) that Peggy Sue would even refuse that one; she's a golden who likes to recycle food. He rolled his eyes and said "the list again" (G). He is learning that we are a neat (1960s word) community that shares *all* that is golden.

Anyway, to continue, Peggy Sue, there were also "sections" of seaweed and shells. I don't know if they retained their fishy smell as I didn't get that close. I apologize for that, but I did think about you.

Thanks for the thought—been there, done that. One "memorable" trip to the beach was somewhat amusing, depending on your location. Had a 1978 VW pop-top at the time. Took the girls for their first real beach trip; they saw the open expanse of sand and got really excited. Also ran around like Pac-Man on high speed gobbling sand and whatever else. Mistake. That night, both dogs had the trots. Thought all was well when we went to bed. Becky in the top bunk, next to me. Michael and The Pigger down below. 5:00 a.m. awakened by Becky doing the UUMMphh—UUMMpphh—UUUrrrpp I'm gonna puke thing. I'm in my bag, yelling at Michael "get the towels." No fool, Michael opted to stay under cover until the problem, er, cleared itself. Ugly mess, but we lived through it. Life's a beach, eh?

146

Becky (Boy, that was embarrassing. I didn't eat any more junk on the beach until the next day.)

Peggy Sue (Wow! I'm impressed! Target vomiting—wonder if I can learn that?)

Earnie (Wish I'da been there for that. Maybe next time. chewchewpeechewchewpeesleeppooppeechew)

Michael & Scotty Richardson
The Golden Gang
Becky: The Red Scourge of Squirrels, Feline Track Coach
Peggy Sue: Pixie, Lover of Every Creature, Fecal Gourmet
Earnie: aka Small White Shark, Grass Gobbler, Teddy Snatcher

FLYING LESSON?

Peggy Sue has been teaching Earnie to fly. Actually, he learned in one lesson. Included in the lesson was the fact that a twelve-pound golden is no match for a sixty-pound golden. He learns fast. Peggy Sue decided Earnie is fun to play with and vice versa. Peggy Sue is on one end of the yard, Earnie on the other. Peggy Sue runs at Earnie. Earnie runs at Peggy Sue. Thud. Earnie flies through the air, lands on his back, and relocates to the underside of the picnic table, safe from Peggy Sue. I *swear* Pigger was grinning!

Becky (Typical. Two dumb blondes. Just about what you'd expect.)
Peggy Sue (Watch this! I'm on the forty, the thirty, the ten—TOUCHDOWN!)
Earnie (I CAN FLYYYYYYYYY! *OOF* THUD ouchouchouch didja get the number of that truck?)

Michael & Scotty Richardson
The Golden Gang
Becky: The Red Scourge of Squirrels, Feline Track Coach
Peggy Sue: Pixie, Lover of Every Creature, Fecal Gourmet
Earnie: aka Small White Shark, Grass Gobbler, Teddy Snatcher

THIN-SKINNED—SORRY!

Wow! I had no idea the post I sent yesterday would get such a reaction. First, let me apologize for being thin-skinned. I shouldn't have let anybody get to me like that. Usually, I ignore posts that irritate me or get nasty. I also sometimes ignore threads that "beat a dead horse" to the point of nausea. There's a big difference between healthy debate and some of what we've seen here on the list lately. My opinion, just my opinion.

At this writing, it has been twenty-four hours since I posted, and I have received over 110 letters both privately and publicly encouraging me not to leave the list. I have not received a single negative reply. That's pushing 10 percent of the list. Amazing. Thank all of you for your support; it's flattering. I sincerely hope that my coming uncorked a bit will help other listers to think about what they are saying and *how* they say it before they hit the send key. Things that are meant to be humorous can be misinterpreted, as we cannot see the look on your face when you write them.

Egos can get out of hand. Please think about who you may offend before you hit "send."

This hasn't been a good week here. Mother had a stroke. Best friend died suddenly. Then yesterday I had a run-in with our new neighbor who threatened to "make meat" out of Becky because she wandered six feet onto his two-and-one-half-acre lot. The previous neighbors encouraged her to visit them, and trying to convince her that she can no longer cross the property line on that side of the house is tough. As you can imagine, this type of a threat to my no. 1 dog upsets me severely. I explained to the neighbor in a shaky voice that any harm to my dogs would be a *big* mistake as I would then have to make a "project" out of him. He apologized, but the harm is done. I no longer can feel comfortable with Becky outside near his property.

On the positive side, Becky has begun to soften her stance on Earnie. She now drinks from the same water bowl as him, and yesterday, she actually allowed him to lie next to her for a nap. This is going to work! Again, I thank all of you who wrote in support of my posts. It means a lot to me, and I hope this will set a new more positive, gentler tone to the list. The list is a real gift, literally. Thank you, Wade. Please don't pull the plug. Common sense will prevail.

Becky (What'd that guy mean, "make meat" out of me? I thought he liked me. He petted me?)

Peggy Sue (Well, it's common knowledge you're a meat head. Maybe it has something to do with that.)

Earnie (I am *so* happy! I got to lie down with the *big* dogs! Am I a member of the pack yet?)

Michael & Scotty Richardson
The Golden Gang
Becky: The Red Scourge of Squirrels, Feline Track Coach
Peggy Sue: Pixie, Lover of Every Creature, Fecal Gourmet
Earnie: aka Small White Shark, Grass Gobbler, Teddy Snatcher

A HAIRY BRIGHT IDEA?

Warning: This post may not be deemed "serious" by some! (Disclaimer)

The post about the dog looking as if it had exploded in the kitchen from blowing coat gave me an idea. I've always been an idea man. For over thirty years casting a certain glance at my wife elicits the same response: "Don't get any bright ideas, Buster!" I've always wondered who Buster is.

On to the subject: golden hair! First, we need to know the types of dog hair. Puppy hair. This is finer than frog hair, in case you may have forgotten. It gets in the eyes, the nostrils, the ears, and your food. If unchecked, it works itself to your heart. This causes a condition known as "ain'thecuteitus" which manifests itself by giving you a warm fuzzy feeling around puppies. Not fatal, but distracting. Perhaps Dr. Jim would be willing to give medical details on this condition. Then there's plain old dog hair. My question is: why fight it? If all the money we spend on cleaning equipment were used for golden rescue! Think of it! Besides, golden hair is an excellent insulator. We spend exorbitant amounts of dollars on wall-to-wall carpets. Why? If you have three goldens, as we do, the floor will be totally covered with gorgeous *free* hair in no time! The dog hair will be self-limiting; you tall folks will notice it's getting easier to reach the ceiling. Time to get the grass rake out and bag up some free insulation! Put it in the walls, the attic! Those of you with more dogs can send hair to people in colder climates. All the money saved on insulation can be used for Rescue Dogs! History shows us that the English (those dogs!) lived with their livestock for heat. I think this should work! If you relax with the hair, pretty soon it won't bother you.

Case in point: the old Hairmobile. The longer we drove it, the quieter it got. We wondered why, until we sold it and had to clean it out. We thought it had carpets! Imagine the surprise when we found rubber floor mats under the dog hair! The added insulation provided by the dog hair quieted the engine sounds! What do you think?

Becky (I think another blonde in the house has caused you to inhale too much blonde fur—it's known that blonde fur causes brain damage!)
Peggy Sue (Hmmm. Would this mean I could use the "rug" for my burritos?)
Earnie (Here, Dad, inhale some more puppy hair!)

Michael & Scotty Richardson
The Golden Gang
Becky: The Red Scourge of Squirrels, Feline Track Coach
Peggy Sue: Pixie, Lover of Every Creature, Fecal Gourmet
Earnie: aka Small White Shark, Grass Gobbler, Teddy Snatcher

GOLDEN FEELINGS?

I can say with all certainty—*yes,* goldens have feelings. I know because last night, Earnie chewed on Peggy Sue's tail while she was napping. Didn't know she could bellow that loud.

Becky (What *are* we going to do with that puppy? He's like a festering sore—can I street-train him? Here, Earnie, let me show you a bus! Heh heh!)
Peggy Sue (Yow! Next time you do that, you little pistol, I'll make chowder out of ya!)
Earnie (Well, it was lying right next to my chew rope. How was I supposed to know? What a couple of old bitches anyway!)

Michael & Scotty Richardson
The Golden Gang
Becky: The Red Scourge of Squirrels, Feline Track Coach
Peggy Sue: Pixie, Lover of Every Creature, Fecal Gourmet
Earnie: aka Small White Shark, Grass Gobbler, Teddy Snatcher

BUMP IN THE NIGHT

Earnie is in his third week with us, he's now ten weeks old. He is training us nicely. We could use some advice.

He sleeps in a Vari kennel at the foot of our bed. We had no trouble the first two weeks, other than the initial howling the first couple of nights. Now, however, he has decided he's *not* sleepy when we put him to bed, usually around midnight because I work a swing shift. He thrashes around in the kennel for two to three hours. He sounds just like our cat did when she fell asleep in the dryer and Michael turned it on. THUMP! WHUMP! THUD! (No harm to the kitty, other than dizziness) He flings himself from end to end.

Very little vocal stuff, just this constant bumping and banging. Needless to say we are *not* sleeping well. It has been suggested we should kennel him in another area of the house. I hate to do that; the girls sleep in our room, and I think he needs the company. We are feeding him three times daily: 7:00 a.m.,1:00 p.m., 7:00 p.m. Should we move his feeding schedule? Is he hungry? We also cut off his water at about 10:00 p.m., to avoid accidents in the night. Should he have more water? Could he be thirsty? Should we follow him the last four hours before bedtime and poke him in the butt if he tries to sleep? (Just kidding!) I still take him out in the night, usually around 4:00 a.m. He always pees, never has to do no. 2 (see, I didn't use the poop word!). Any suggestions by the wise people on the list would be appreciated. Sleep deprivation is setting in.

Becky (I *told* ya he was gonna be a pain. Hey, Earnie, have you seen Dad's brush shredder? Look at this hole in this end, right here—closer, closer, hehhehheh!)

Peggy Sue (Hey he's my playmate! But he *does* wear me out!)

Earnie (So it's 2:00 a.m.? So what? Let's boogie!)

Michael & Scotty Richardson
The Golden Gang
Becky: The Red Scourge of Squirrels, Feline Track Coach
Peggy Sue: Pixie, Lover of Every Creature, Fecal Gourmet
Earnie: aka Small White Shark, Grass Gobbler, Teddy Snatcher

HUMP IN THE NIGHT?

A big *THANK YOU* to all who responded to our plea for help with our newest
golden child—Earnie. We took the advice of at least two of you immediately (because it was quick and easy!). One suggestion was to put a *big* woobie in the crate with him. We did this with a bit of apprehension, as he, er, seems to like humping the bigger woobies during play. I dunno how *that* would sound in the middle of the night :-)!
However, it seemed to calm him right down when he cuddled up to the *Big
Bear* woobie. The other suggestion was to cover the crate. At the 4:00 a.m. potty break, he was restless after I returned him to the Vari kennel, so I covered the crate with my robe (just the front of the crate, no ventilation problem), and once again he settled down and actually slept through the remainder of the night! There are many other suggestions that are well worth trying if these things don't continue to do the trick. I love this list! Ah sleep! It feels good to be rested again!
BTW, Peggy Sue and Earnie play throughout the evening, so he gets little chance to rest. Perhaps this will help wear the little bugger out. Becky continues to be the ultimate bitch; she nailed Earnie good this a.m. (no blood) when he used her head for traction. :-(

Becky (What we have here, see, is a *respect* problem. You know, "R-E-S-P-E-C-T!" as in the Aretha Franklin tune!)
Peggy Sue (I don't think we have a respect problem. I think we have a bitchy redhead problem. Blondes rule!)
Earnie (Ow! She bit me! Guess I'll go hump a woobie—)

Michael & Scotty Richardson
The Golden Gang
Becky: The Red Scourge of Squirrels, Feline Track Coach
Peggy Sue: Pixie, Lover of Every Creature, Fecal Gourmet
Earnie: aka Small White Shark, Grass Gobbler, Teddy Snatcher

MR. MEANIE?

We could use some advice from people who have gone through raising a pup with two older dogs. Earnie, our twelve-week-old golden "son" is getting too rough in his play with Peggy Sue. Pigger, as we call her, is the *world's most gentle golden.* She is getting the worst of play sessions between her and Earnie. Pigger will initiate the play, and obviously enjoys it, rolling about the floor feinting, biting, growling until Earnie gets too worked up. Earnie will get a bit frantic at which point he turns into "Mr. Snapper." On one occasion, he perforated the Pigger's ear. She wouldn't play with him for three days afterwards. Now she's playing with him again, but if it gets too rough she literally will jump on your lap or the picnic table to avoid the *pup from hell* until he calms down. We are attempting to discourage some of this rough play, but Earnie gets monomaniacal sometimes. He knows better than to try it with Becky; she took a fall out of him, and he keeps a respectful distance from her unless she wants to play with him. Should we rescue The Pigger or just let it go? Will she eventually lay the big bite on the little turd, or will she always defer to him? Egad, puppies are fun! :-(

Becky (Hey I told you we should have run him through the Cuisinart. Now he's too big. How about the trash compactor?)
Peggy Sue (Get that little (*%^*&^)(^ away from me! OW my ear! I don't want pierced ears!)
Earnie (Grrrrrrr! Gonna getcha! Pantpant runrun run bite jump snarl fast as fast can be, you'll never catch me!)

Michael & Scotty Richardson
The Golden Gang
Becky: The Red Scourge of Squirrels, Feline Track Coach
Peggy Sue: Pixie, Lover of Every Creature, Fecal Gourmet
Earnie: aka Small White Shark, Grass Gobbler, Teddy Snatcher

EARNIE'S BIG DAY!

Earnie got his first taste of the forest today! At the ripe old age of twelve weeks, he accompanied us on a field trip Michael and I led for the purpose of collecting and identifying wild mushrooms. We *almost* kenneled him, but Michael reminded me that Peggy Sue was introduced to hiking trails at about his age. Peggy Sue is the world's best hiking buddy. She never gets more than a few feet away from us; she never needs a lead in these remote areas. By starting Earnie out at this age we hope to train him to be a good, reliable hiker as well.

Earnie had a ball! He was far less trouble than we anticipated. He is used to riding in the truck; we have been taking him for short rides from the age of eight weeks. He rides in the cab with us, and Peggy Sue and Becky occupy the canopy-covered rear. We have a pass-through window so they can drool on us, and so Earnie can check on the big dogs by standing on his hind legs and looking through the window. We started him with a flexi-lead on the trail, and after a couple of miles, we tried him off-lead. No problem. He never wandered more than ten feet from us the whole day. Our dogs wear bear bells so we always know where they are. Earnie chewed sticks, dug holes, and in general, just enjoyed himself. He also got his first swimming lesson, somewhat by accident. Becky and The Pigger were playing in a creek when he decided it looked like fun—so in he went! He looked a bit surprised, but swam to shore with no difficulty. He managed to shake water on us just like the *big* dogs do! Earnie is learning to be a true golden—loves the forests, fields, and streams. For the record, this was a great day for 'shrooming— perhaps Earnie is good luck? Except for the rain! It poured buckets on us all afternoon. Being a typical golden, Earnie loves the rain and should be required to wear a "dangerous when wet" sign. Being wet really fires him up! All in all, a golden day.

Becky (I think the little squirt might work out OK! I taught him how to carry sticks up the trail and hit the old folks behind the knees!)
Peggy Sue (I showed him how to roll in the moss and dig holes and swim!)
Earnie (The woods are a *great* place to go! Look at all those sticks to chew! And creeks to play in! And some of those old-growth trees were ten feet in diameter! Wow, really neato places to pee!)

Michael & Scotty Richardson
The Golden Gang
Becky: The Red Scourge of Squirrels, Feline Track Coach
Peggy Sue: Pixie, Lover of Every Creature, Fecal Gourmet
Earnie: aka Small White Shark, Grass Gobbler, Teddy Snatcher

DOGS IN THE WILDERNESS

I'm sure this will get me flamed by some of the more conservative list members—but I feel the need to inject my two cents worth. Having spent *a lot* of time over the last sixteen years in the woods with my dogs, I think I'm qualified to speak on the subject. We have backpacked, camped, hiked, canoed, mushroomed, swam, etc., *extensively* and included the dogs wherever we could. If the situation calls for your dog to be on a lead, and if that increases your comfort level, put the dog on a lead. Michael and I usually try to take our dogs where they will not be a problem to others if they are off lead. Here in the NW, we have a lot of little-used spots where we can hike and hunt mushrooms and not see another person all day. The biggest problem this time of the year is hunters. It is perfectly legal to shoot a dog harassing wildlife in this area. Becky has a deer-chasing problem, so if we are in units heavily populated with deer, and the hunting season is open, we leash her. Peggy Sue never leaves our side. She needs no leash in the woods. Deer have walked to within twenty feet of her, and she merely stands and watches them. We are hoping to train Earnie to react the same as Pigger. Start the dog young, and make the woods a familiar part of their lives. By making your dogs familiar with the forest, they won't go nuts on you when you take them with you backpacking. As for danger from wild animals—excuse me, but—phooey! The most dangerous things in the woods walk on *two legs*. Our girls wear bear bells (always!) when in the wilderness. We have never had an encounter with a "dangerous" animal. Skunks and porcupines are rare in this area. But rarely fatal, if encountered, anyway. Wild animals will stay away from you except in *rare* cases. If you're crazy enough to take you and your dogs in a grizzly area, well common sense should enter into the equation somewhere, shouldn't it?

Sure everybody can tell a story about encounters with animals in the forest, but whose fault was it? The animals? I doubt it. Usually, it's because the human involved did something stupid. I'd far rather take my chances in the wilderness than in the Chicago or LA 'burbs. So this weekend, we will probably go 'shroom hunting again—with our dogs. Flame away!

Becky (I love the woods! Mushroom hunting is my favorite activity!)
Peggy Sue (Me too! I'm the world's finest trail companion!)
Earnie (I wanna go too! There's lots of good sniffs out there!)

Michael & Scotty Richardson
The Golden Gang
Becky: The Red Scourge of Squirrels, Feline Track Coach
Peggy Sue: Pixie, Lover of Every Creature, Fecal Gourmet
Earnie: aka Small White Shark, Grass Gobbler, Teddy Snatcher

HMMMM—YOUR DOGS' DIET?

After hanging on every word of the food discussions (yes, really!) I decided to discuss the subject with my girls. The comments about the diet of wild canids and feral dogs came up. Peggy Sue and Becky offered these golden comments: If you let dogs eat what they want to eat, without humans butting in with their ideas of what is good for dogs! Think about it! What is *your* dogs' favorite food? Is it the Eagle, or Iams, or some other expensive concoction? Of course not! Try this test: Put a bowl of your
human idea of what's good for your dog (Purina, Iams, Eagle, etc.) next to a pile of horse manure, cow manure, wild blackberries, huckleberries, dirt clods, dead fish, underwear, socks, blankets, green grass, etc. All together now—what did your pampered pooch go for? Uh huh, just as we thought! Remember now, the wild canids had no humans to tell them horse poop was a poor diet and bad for their coats. But they survived! If you read the book, *The Intelligence of Dogs,* by Stanley Coren you will find that the feral dogs of old ate much worse than the above items. Corpses were thrown off the walls of cities, and dogs survived on those. So I guess the dogs did eat meat, but some of us may never know if what they ate tastes like the chicken or lamb we now feed them. Personally, I have never dined on a fellow human. But then, I've never eaten dog either. Perhaps we're missing something here?

Becky (All right! Does this mean I can go back to my diet of elk poop?)
Peggy Sue (You *know* what I like!)
Earnie (Are all female dogs as disgusting as you two? Whadda ya mean, try it, you'll like it?)

Michael & Scotty Richardson
The Golden Gang
Becky: The Red Scourge of Squirrels, Feline Track Coach
Peggy Sue: Pixie, Lover of Every Creature, Fecal Gourmet
Earnie: aka Small White Shark, Grass Gobbler, Teddy Snatcher

SNOW BRAINER?

Earnie, our precocious thirteen-week-old golden, has had another life-altering experience. He's seen snow! Took him along with the rest of our "pack" for a Chanterelle hunt about fifty miles from here. It has snowed in W Washington in the last few days. We didn't expect snow at the mushroom site as it's fairly low—only 2,400 feet elevation. Guess what. Quite a lot of snow, particularly hanging on the big fir trees. Not so much that we couldn't scratch around for mushrooms (found fifty pounds!) but enough to fall out of the trees and smack you on the head hard enough to cause you to see stars. My friend always calls these headache balls of snow "snow-brainers." The older dogs are used to snow falling on them; they *love* snow! Earnie had never even seen snow, much less been half-buried in a large blob of it. The first time he got smacked with a load of snow, he was sure the sky was falling.

After a while, he just took it in stride and played in the lumps after they fell off the trees. True golden temperament. I don't know about all goldens, but snow makes our dogs *crazy!* They roll in it, they eat it, they charge about with reckless abandon. Too much fun! Sort of a whole day of the type of behavior you get immediately after a bath. We all got home wet, cold, and tired—but what a great day! Earnie is becoming "king of the woods" in a hurry! A bonus of these trips is the fact that Earnie and the girls are quite laid back for a couple of days! (VBG)

Becky (Didja see me run down the trail full speed at Earnie, put on the brakes, and slide into him? I rolled the little begger down the snowy hillside! Hehhehheh!)
Peggy Sue (I LOVE SNOW! NOTHING makes me as nuts as snow! Rollrollrollslideeatroll)

Earnie (What *is* this white stuff? Why are the girls rolling in it? Hey, this stuff tastes good! But the sky is falling!)

Michael & Scotty Richardson
The Golden Gang
Becky: The Red Scourge of Squirrels, Feline Track Coach
Peggy Sue: Pixie, Lover of Every Creature, Fecal Gourmet
Earnie: aka Small White Shark, Grass Gobbler, Teddy Snatcher

DOGGIE DIETS? YUCK

At 11:39 p.m.—0700 10/21/96, Tom wrote:
Hi Golden Friends,

I have a friend that has two mature goldens. Both dogs are very healthy. He has asked me to ask you all if there is any way to stop your golden from eating poop. I kinda thought that there is an enzyme that you can add to their food that makes the poop unpalatable. Does anyone know of this, or any other way to stop a cute golden for from being a poop eater?

Well, now, I guess this is a subject we are experts on. Peggy Sue (aka Fecal
Gourmet) has proven unstoppable. We have read every behavior book we can get our hands on. Adolph's Meat Tenderizer was supposed to stop it. Peggy Sue said, "Mmmmmm! Tender turds!" Spinach mixed with the food—Peggy Sue said, "Mmmm! I feel strong, like Popeye!" Tabasco sauce applied liberally to the turf tacos—Peggy Sue said, "Mmmmmm! Mexican!" I could go on and on—but you get the point, right? The only sure cure we have found is to closely follow her with the pooper-scooper and "get it while it's hot!" She *is* the fecal gourmet and only eats her own product. Nobody else's is edible, as applied to dog poop. Elk poop, deer poop, etc.—OK. Perhaps it's the nice round little nurbles, somewhat reminiscent of her dried kibble dog food? Of course we haven't fed her too many things shaped like horse turds, and *those* are a real delicacy. Go figure.

Becky (I don't do doggy doo—but gotta admit, those Elk droppings are to die for!)

Peggy Sue (One bad habit, just one—big deal!)
Earnie (I couldn't believe my eyes! Did you *see* what my ever-so-ladylike
sister was eating? Yuk!)

Michael & Scotty Richardson
The Golden Gang
Becky: The Red Scourge of Squirrels, Feline Track Coach
Peggy Sue: Pixie, Lover of Every Creature, Fecal Gourmet
Earnie: Marriage Test, Becky's Best Buddy, Chewin' Machine

MASS WOOBICIDE?

Earnie, our fourteen-week-old golden boy, has developed a taste for Woobie guts.

Woobies the girls have known and loved for years are dying like flies. He never met a Woobie he couldn't disembowel. Woobies that enter his kennel (aka The Lair) at bedtime shaped like Luciano Pavarotti emerge in the morning resembling Richard Simmons. The yard is decorated with tube-shaped cotton balls. This guy reminds me of those wind-up teeth you used to buy at carnivals—twenty pounds of teeth at high speed. Yack—like Pac-Man on amphetamines. He *ate* the filling (polyester) from a teddy bear which died a horrible death in his kennel. Don't know what the nutritional value of polyester is, but it makes nice lawn decorations. Ah puppies. Arrggghhh!

Becky (He's killing all our toys! Time for a garage sale run for some fresh woobies!)
Peggy Sue (What's this white stuff on the lawn? Hmmmm!)
Earnie (C'mon, Mr. Teddy Bear—share my condo for the night! Heh heh heh!)

Michael & Scotty Richardson
The Golden Gang
Becky: The Red Scourge of Squirrels, Feline Track Coach
Peggy Sue: Pixie, Lover of Every Creature, Fecal Gourmet
Earnie: Marriage Test, Becky's Best Buddy, Chewin' Machine

THE PIDDLEOMETER?

Arrrghh! Puppies! Just when you think they're housebroken, they present you with a nice wet surprise. You're walking barefoot across the living room carpet and—squish! You step on the *wet* spot. You don't remember letting the pestilent pupper out of your sight long enough to pee the rug.

When did that happen? Earnie had five (!) perfect days behind him. Today he scored a 9.5 on the piddleometer. For those of you who don't know what a piddleometer is, it's a device similar to a rain gauge expressly designed to rate your success at housebreaking your pup. Don't bother looking at Petco, these are a special order item available from Peggy Sue Enterprises, also known as Waste Recyclers Inc. OK out there—when did *your* puppy become *perfect* in his/her housebreaking? BTW, Mom always said I wasn't real easy to train, either—

Becky (Boy, ya gotta be real careful where ya lay down around here. I like mud puddles, but this, this is a pi**er!)

Peggy Sue (Hey I've got a bad habit or two, but at least I take it outside before I recycle it.)

Earnie (Well, it seemed the thing to do at the time. When ya gotta go—ya gotta go!)

Michael & Scotty Richardson
The Golden Gang
Becky: The Red Scourge of Squirrels, Feline Track Coach
Peggy Sue: Pixie, Lover of Every Creature, Fecal Gourmet
Earnie: Marriage Test, Becky's Best Buddy, Chewin' Machine

GIMMEE A BRAKE?

Earnie, our fourteen-week-old golden child, has learned another cute (?) little trick. He's learned to run and jump. So what, you say? One little problem—his running and jumping are things he does well, but he hasn't yet learned to stop. His judgment is a *bit* off when it comes to how far he's going to travel after he applies his brakes. Last night, he charged out of the laundry room at warp speed. He picked up a little steam in the end of the family room. He then leaped onto the futon, slid all the way across my lap, and onto the end table, causing several remote controllers and a *full* Pepsi to make a short trip to the floor. He ended that little excursion with his front end dangling off the end table and his butt in my face. I looked at Michael, and we both *cracked up*. How do you get mad at something so danged cute?

Becky (I was *so* sure he was gonna get it!)
Peggy Sue (Yeah, I guess I should have warned you guys. He runs into the chain link fence too.)
Earnie (Huffhuffhuffhuff here I COME! Get ready—oooooof! Sorry!)

Michael & Scotty Richardson
The Golden Gang
Becky: The Red Scourge of Squirrels, Feline Track Coach
Peggy Sue: Pixie, Lover of Every Creature, Fecal Gourmet
Earnie: Marriage Test, Becky's Best Buddy, Chewin' Machine

KAMIKAZE PUPPER?

Earnie continues to make us age faster. According to our manual on puppies, he's in an assertive-aggressive stage for the next couple of weeks. Quote:
"During this period he may become assertive and somewhat domineering in an attempt to find his place in the pack." This is breeder-speak for "Earnie's going to be a bit of an a**hole for a week or two. If you live through this stage, read the next chapter." This morning he learned how to dive-bomb
Becky. She is *not amused*. He gathered speed across the family room, leaped onto the futon, and launched himself at her, landing squarely on her head. I would be interested if someone could explain the physiology making it possible for a sixty-pound golden to let out a roar the size of the one that came out of Becky. It even scared me. It deterred Earnie for, oh about five minutes or so too. Puppies—arrggghhh!

Becky (Try that one more time, kid, and you're gonna be a eunuch!)
Peggy Sue (Uh, oh, Earnie, I wouldn't do that if I were you. She can be a real bitch!)
Earnie (Huffhuffhuff I can flyyyyyyyy! Hahahahahah gotcha, Becky!)

Michael & Scotty Richardson
The Golden Gang
Becky: The Red Scourge of Squirrels, Feline Track Coach
Peggy Sue: Pixie, Lover of Every Creature, Fecal Gourmet
Earnie: Marriage Test, Becky's Best Buddy, Chewin' Machine

TASTLESS HUMOR?

The recent discussion on feeding fresh meats to our goldens got me to thinking. Actually, the unwanted solicitors knocking on our door helped with this idea. I believe I have a great *idea* for an endless supply of meat to feed our dogs. Of course, the supply may dwindle somewhat in the off-election years. But there are always a few religious zealots, insurance salesmen, lost motorists, etc. bound to knock on your door from time to time. How about those guys in suits riding bicycles all over your neighborhood trying to convert you to their religion? Ever wonder how they taste? A bonus of this variety of meat is it should be pretty free of parasites. Unless you count the whole organism as a parasite. I guess care should be taken not to feed the dogs a steady diet of insurance sales persons, as they will surely develop an attitude over time. Variety is the key here. A few Republicans, a liberal or two, the occasional Avon Lady! And for those of you who don't have a stomach for this sort of thing, and insist on feeding kibble-based diets—there's always Soylent Green!

Becky (Dad, you better hope there aren't too many insurance sales persons on the list!)
Peggy Sue (I notice people come in different colors and shapes. Do they taste different too?)
Earnie (Just my luck. I bet none of the rest of my litter went to a whacko household.)

Michael & Scotty Richardson
The Golden Gang
Becky: The Red Scourge of Squirrels, Feline Track Coach
Peggy Sue: Pixie, Lover of Every Creature, Fecal Gourmet
Earnie: Marriage Test, Becky's Best Buddy, Chewin' Machine

EARNIE'S EXCELLENT WEEKEND!

Earnie, now at fourteen weeks, has had his first big weekend of socialization. My wife has worked seventeen years on the Catlin Gabel Rummage sale, the biggest sale of its kind west of the Mississippi. Thousands of people come from all over for this four-day event. It's held in a huge Exposition Center in Portland, Oregon. What better place to see how Earnie reacts to crowds and hullaballoo?

Off to the sale, pup on lead! In the door, where ten (at least) people swoop down upon the cute puppy to fondle him. He did what I would have done. He peed. Arrgghh, thinks I—this isn't going to work. Wrong! After the initial shock of being the no. 1 attraction, he *absolutely* loved it. No fear! Huge carts we move rummage on were rolling in the isles, folks dragging big cardboard boxes, etc. No problem. Hundreds of people petted him. He even rode on top of the rummage carts while we moved stuff around, tail wagging. Pretty cute, like a captain on the bow of his ship. No other accidents; we spent three days there, and he always made it outside to the grass. Of course, the next day, he piddled all over the new car. Nobody's perfect. But he's close!

Becky (Why didn't *I* get to go? I love that kind of stuff! Danged kid, anyhow.)

Peggy Sue (Not me, nope, don't wanna go there. Cardboard boxes scare the crap out of me. And killer carts? No way, Jose!)

Earnie (Ohhhh look at all the hands to pet me! And I got to shop in the toy section and pick out new woobies every day! That was the best part—thousands and thousands of woobies!)

Michael & Scotty Richardson
The Golden Gang
Becky: The Red Scourge of Squirrels, Feline Track Coach
Peggy Sue: Pixie, Lover of Every Creature, Fecal Gourmet
Earnie: Marriage Test, Becky's Best Buddy, Chewin' Machine

AGE OF DESTRUCTION?

(Insert belly laugh here!) Are there *really* folks out there naive enough to think *any* amount of training will keep their sweet golden puppy from annihilating rugs, furniture, drapes, underwear, bedspreads, etc.? No matter how well you train 'em, they'll find something to get into. Earnie is now at four months. He's housebroken (finally, we hope) but he's in a fierce chewing stage. New teeth are arriving, gotta chew.

He's laying under my chair as I write gnawing on a Dentabone. He sneaks a little taste of the chair leg occasionally as if I can't feel the grinding.

If I left him alone for *five* minutes, I should expect disaster. He needs constant supervision, inside or out, and he's getting it. Still, he gets a piece of the shrubs while passing by, a mouthful of dirt or grass on a potty run, and always scores a fir cone or leaf of some sort to bring in the house and chew up. While playing with the other dogs, puppy exuberance kicks in, and he grabs a mouthful of carpet. All the woobies are being systematically gutted. He poops kapok and polyester fill. He eats bugs. Barkdust. Lord knows what he eats on our mushroom hunting trips. I watch carefully, but all you need to do is bend over to pick a 'shroom, and when you stand up he's got *something* in his mouth. Ah puppies. Peggy Sue demolished several sets of VW seat belts before she outgrew the puppy stage. They're replaceable. Peggy Sue isn't. This too, shall pass. :-(

Becky (I am the perfect dog. I never destroyed anything!)
Peggy Sue (Yeah well, you were a year old when you arrived. I needed to screw stuff up or the folks would have thought I had something wrong with me.)

Earnie (HA! Gutted another woobie! *Love* the way the stuffing comes out in a long string, tastes great, less filling! ChewchewchewdigchewpeerunharassPeggySue)

Michael & Scotty Richardson
The Golden Gang
Becky: The Red Scourge of Squirrels, Feline Track Coach
Peggy Sue: Pixie, Lover of Every Creature, Fecal Gourmet
Earnie: Marriage Test, Becky's Best Buddy, Chewin' Machine

FUTON BANDITO

Add this to the growing list of cute (?) things our puppers do—Earnie has learned that when the phone rings, he can dive on the futon and Michael cannot reach him. So he digs, cavorts, and generally enjoys himself until she's off the phone—then he jumps off knowing he's about to get physically removed. The futon and *all* the furniture is off limits to him. Except when the phone rings. This clown is only four months old. What are we going to do when he gets older and smarter? We're getting older, but no smarter.

Trouble ahead, eh?

Becky (I told you to take him back months ago, didn't I?)
Peggy Sue (The futon is mine, dang it. Get that pestilent puke off my napping spot!)
Earnie (Fast as fast can beeeee—you can't catch me! RunrunpantpantrunharassPeggySue)

Michael & Scotty Richardson
The Golden Gang
Becky: The Red Scourge of Squirrels, Feline Track Coach
Peggy Sue: Pixie, Lover of Every Creature, Fecal Gourmet
Earnie: Marriage Test, Becky's Best Buddy, Chewin' Machine

WHOS THERE?

Love the destruction thread, got a lot of laughs! Now, a quiz for those of you raising a puppy. Does your pup exhibit several distinct personalities? Earnie has several modes.

1. Lover boy. This is the most common mode, best observed right after a nap, or after being sprung from his crate when we had to leave him for a while. Snuggles, talks, rolls over for tummy rub, soft as butter.
2. The Lone Haranguer. Becky and The Pigger really hate this one. He's bored, so they're expected to put up with his chasing, woobie snatching, toy thieving, biting, barking, and general harassment.
3. Mr. Snapper. During this personality switch, he becomes a real tough guy. Snaps at everything with audible whacking sound, including Michael and I as well as the girls. Mild correction required here if you want to be wearing clothes after this mood passes. Has already ruined one of Michael's favorite skirts. Full of little holes, looks like shot with buckshot.
4. Holy Terror. Runs about the house, warp 9 or faster, biting everything, ricocheting off tables, chairs, Becky, Peggy Sue, my legs, etc. Fails to negotiate turn into kitchen, slides across linoleum floor on backside. Humps woobies, Peggy Sue, tries to hump Becky (so far a dangerous and unsuccessful endeavor), and is eventually reined in by Becky who knocks him down and gives him a few "nose jabs" for good measure.
5. Sleeping. This is one of my favorites, as well as a favorite of Becky and The Pigger. Ah puppies!

Becky (He tries to hump me *one more time* and he's not gonna need to go to the vets to get neutered!)

Peggy Sue (Ha! Now Becky has two blondes to deal with! Blondes rule!)

Earnie (Hahahahahaha! Here comes Mr. Snapper, fast as fast can beeeeee!

You'll never get meeeee! Ooof! Hey, Becky, that hurt! Oof! Oof!)

Michael & Scotty Richardson
The Golden Gang
Becky: The Red Scourge of Squirrels, Feline Track Coach
Peggy Sue: Pixie, Lover of Every Creature, Fecal Gourmet
Earnie: Marriage Test, Becky's Best Buddy, Chewin' Machine

WHY EAT POOP?

Because it's there. And I like it. I like it warm. It's really great frozen. Poopsicles. I like it with spinach. I like it with meat tenderizer. I like it with hot sauce. I like it with pepper. If you add salt, I like it even better. I don't like it when you keep the yard sh—, er, spotless. For those of you who think we poop-eaters eat poop because there's something missing from our diets—you're right. Poop is missing from our diets. If they made it in tablets and sold it at the pet store, would you feel better about it?

Signed: Peggy Sue, Fecal Gourmet

Becky (You are sooo revolting. I like dead fish, dead moles, sticks, human poop, but I simply cannot imagine eating dog poop.)
Peggy Sue (There's just no accounting for some other dogs tastes. After all, I *am* the Fecal Gourmet!)
Earnie (Just my luck to end up in a house with a sicko sister—phew! You could use a breath mint, Pigger!)

Michael & Scotty Richardson
The Golden Gang
Becky: The Red Scourge of Squirrels, Feline Track Coach
Peggy Sue: Pixie, Lover of Every Creature, Fecal Gourmet
Earnie: Marriage Test, Becky's Best Buddy, Chewin' Machine

EARNIE'S BIG DAY

Hallelujah! The quarantine is over! For the last three months, we have not allowed any of the dogs out of our yard because of the parvovirus epidemic here in the NW. Now Earnie has had all his shots, we can feel a little safer. Putting it mildly, we were *all* getting booorrreeed. Yawn. Record rains here again this year, and the field behind the house is flooded. This field is Becky and The Pigger's absolute favorite spot to retrieve tennis balls whacked 100 yards or so out into the field, through the water. This was Earnie's first trip into the fields and trails below the house. He was pretty excited! When I began whacking tennis balls with my Spalding racket, and Becky (aka the Red Rocket) romped, swam, and charged through the mud to find them, he was absolutely mystified. Peggy Sue charged off in hot pursuit of a ball. Earnie was still mystified. Plus, why are those two fools running through all that mud and water and getting all wet? Earnie didn't catch on to the long retrieves, but by throwing tennis balls short distances, he knew what to do. The problem with that is this: You *must* be sure Becky doesn't see the tennis ball leave your hand, as she would run through fire, razor blades, broken glass, and over the top of Earnie to fetch a ball. The Tank MacNamara of the dog world. Everybody got a great workout. Earnie ran through the fields with the girls off lead with much adolescent enthusiasm, if not much grace. He's still clumsy at five months, all legs. One large benefit of all this is—they're *all* sleeping!

Becky (At last! I thought I had retrieved my *last* tennis ball! Bonsai! Outa my way, suckers!)
Peggy Sue (Hey, Earnie, try to catch me and get my tennis ball out here in this open field! See, you're not so fast, are you? Heeheehee!)

Earnie (Pantpantpuffpuff wow! Lookit that red bitch run! Do you think I'll ever catch her?)

Michael & Scotty Richardson
The Golden Gang
Becky: The Red Scourge of Squirrels, Feline Track Coach
Peggy Sue: Pixie, Lover of Every Creature, Fecal Gourmet
Earnie: Marriage Test, Becky's Best Buddy, Chewin' Machine

THE RED GOBBLER

Had to laugh at the worry last week about goldens being allergic to turkey. Allow me to ease your troubled minds, if your dogs are anything like Becky, goldens are definitely *not* allergic to turkey. Had a crowd here Thanksgiving day, hard to keep track of all the kids, dogs, etc. Our good friends prepared to leave in the evening. These are dog owners, they should have known better—but they took a bunch of the leftover turkey (we had two twenty-four pounders) and placed it in a large plastic bag by the front door. Uh huh, you guessed it, Becky, old garbage gut, sensed a rare opportunity.

Hunger and sneakiness won out over training and fear of getting caught. She probably ate about three pounds before we caught her. Fortunately, it was all carved off the bone so she didn't get poultry bones in her tummy. Ah the guilty look when we spotted that red butt in the air and the head in the bag!

Becky (Well, it *was* on the floor, sort of. Why are you laughing? I thought I was really gonna get it, and you're laughing?)
Peggy Sue (I was able to withstand the temptation. However, had that been a bag of poop, well I just dunno!)
Earnie (OK, so THAT'S how you do it—just wait until I'm bigger, we'll see who gets the bird, Becky!)

Michael & Scotty Richardson
The Golden Gang
Becky: The Red Scourge of Squirrels, Feline Track Coach
Peggy Sue: Pixie, Lover of Every Creature, Fecal Gourmet
Earnie: Marriage Test, Becky's Best Buddy, Chewin' Machine

HAWAIIAN POOP EATER?

This suggestion is for the person that was having problems with a puppy eating its stools. My golden unfortunately has the same problem. A simple solution that I found is to put a little pineapple juice on his food for two or three days. I am not sure why it works, but it does. It usually last for four to eight weeks. If I catch him "snacking" again, I repeat the dosage. Hope this helps.

Tried this with Peggy Sue. Caught her with a hula skirt sipping pineapple daiquiris with her snacks.

Becky (Yeah, The Pigger is a hopeless poop eater—)
Peggy Sue (Don't knock it 'til you try it!)
Earnie (Reeeeppppulllllsivvvve!)

Michael & Scotty Richardson
The Golden Gang
Becky: The Red Scourge of Squirrels, Feline Track Coach
Peggy Sue: Pixie, Lover of Every Creature, Fecal Gourmet
Earnie: Marriage Test, Becky's Best Buddy, Chewin' Machine

JOE CAMEL

Anybody had any experience with this one? Earnie, our six-month-old golden child, had not had an accident in the house for several weeks. Shortly after coming home from the hospital, we noticed he had one in the living room. Another at the end of the hallway where my bedroom is, outside the door. The kicker was when he waltzed into the family room, did not ask to go out, no barking, whining, or any of the usual signs of distress—just tipped up his chin, stretched a bit, and proceeded to piddle a puddle approximately the size (and color) of Lake Erie. He was so engrossed in what he was doing that clapping, shouting, screaming, did nothing. Finally, a well-aimed magazine stopped the flow, by now washing the Presto-Logs off the hearth, and we got him outside where he finished his business.

Upon a bit of investigation, we discovered the water bowl, a large plastic dishpan capable of holding about two gallons of water, was at least two quarts low. This was filled about an hour before. Becky and The Pigger usually drink once, maybe twice a day. We are pretty certain Earnie drank the whole two quarts. Dang. Perhaps what we have here is a golden capable of high desert hunting in the dead of summer. He could accompany camels as they cross the Gobi Desert. If he could hold it. We have since removed the water dish and offer a couple of drinks a day. Does my boy have a drinking problem? He seems fine physically, no bladder problems. Could he be doing this because the cold water feels good on his sore gums? We are giving him a few ice cubes a day, and he just holds them in his mouth. Any suggestions? OK to withhold the water?

Becky (Now you know why he's a soft dog. The little arfer is waterlogged!)
Peggy Sue (I really admired the size of that puddle!)
Earnie (Slurp slurp slurp belch piss drink slurp)

Michael & Scotty Richardson
The Golden Gang
Becky: The Red Scourge of Squirrels, Feline Track Coach
Peggy Sue: Pixie, Lover of Every Creature, Fecal Gourmet
Earnie: Marriage Test, Becky's Best Buddy, Chewin' Machine

WE MAY NEED AN ARK

Golden weather here. I'm sure most of you have been following the ice storms, rain, flooding, snow, etc. we are suffering here in the NW. We have been lucky so far. Haven't lost power. If we do, we are all electric and will have to move into the travel trailer until the power comes on. Took the dogs for our walk this a.m. in full Gore-Tex gear. Us, not the dogs.

Wind, heavy rain, some snow. The trail below the house is impassable, under two feet of water. The big meadow is a lake. The dogs love it. Becky and The Pigger wallow in it, chase sticks, swim, run along the edge of it in a foot of water. Earnie still doesn't see the allure of swimming in ice water. I think he prefers his couch and my lap. Smart dog. Earnie has also learned that if he's off-lead, we can't catch him if he doesn't want to be caught.

Hmmmm. Need some obedience training here. If I weren't so weak from the surgery, I would simply chase him down. Years ago, while jogging with a friend on a ninety-degree day, my Doberman decided we couldn't catch her either. Ha. Chased her for ten miles (no exaggeration!) before she dropped from exhaustion. Grabbed her under her collar, gave her my fiercest look, and told her to come when I called her! She never ran from me again.

Somewhere in her pea brain, she figured I could catch her. Perhaps by summer I will be able to catch the Earnster. By then, we will have done some obedience with him too. Earnie has two baby teeth left, an upper and a lower fang. Too cute! He continues to enjoy his icesockles, seems to ease the teething! Well, gotta go. Better get the boat out just in case. Great weather.

Becky (This *is* great weather! Ice, snow, high water! What could be better?
And ducks, thousands of ducks! Heaven—)
Peggy Sue (Yeah! Way cool! And lots of neat dead stuff always washes up when it floods like this! MMmmmmmmm!)
Earnie (OK, I've seen the lake. Now can we go back to the house? I wanna lie on my couch. You broads are goofy. Women. Humph!)

Michael & Scotty Richardson
The Golden Gang
Becky: The Red Scourge of Squirrels, Feline Track Coach
Peggy Sue: Pixie, Lover of Every Creature, Fecal Gourmet
Earnie: Marriage Test, Becky's Best Buddy, Chewin' Machine

AUTOBIOGRAPHY? HA!

Please say you're kidding. I thought this list was "for the dogs" not the owners. Besides, people such as myself and Shirley MacLaine could not possibly write about all our lives in this short forum. And should I choose to reveal myself, most likely the local or federal law enforcement agencies would find out where I am. Bad news. Keep it light and for our goldens, please. If you want to read autobiographies, buy (or borrow) Newt's book. If you keep a copy of his book around, BTW, syrup of Ipecac isn't necessary. I feel like I wanna puke every time I open the cover.

Becky (Geez, Dad, I thought you said they weren't after you anymore. Statue of limitations, or something.)
Peggy Sue (That's STATUTE, you dummy. Who says blondes are dumb? Is poop-eating illegal?)
Earnie (My hormones are kicking in. Any cute little girl puppers out there wanna write to me? Heeheeheee!)

Michael & Scotty Richardson
The Golden Gang
Becky: The Red Scourge of Squirrels, Feline Track Coach
Peggy Sue: Pixie, Lover of Every Creature, Fecal Gourmet
Earnie: Marriage Test, Becky's Best Buddy, Chewin' Machine

ROCKETMAN?

Thought I'd run this by the list and see if anyone else's pup "suffers" from this syndrome. Earnie is now five and a half months. A perfect (well almost) little gentleman. Easy going, slow moving (except if food is involved), great temperament. He and the girls walk three miles a day on lead and are let off lead in a huge field where I bat tennis balls for them and run them until they (and myself) are exhausted. No lack of exercise for these dogs. Most days, after the walk, the dogs nap. Earnie lacks the hard body and stamina of the girls, being a pup. So he sleeps the most. But with *no* notice—he's lying on the floor, apparently snoozing one moment. His head comes off the carpet. He climbs to his feet. Stretches. And *off he goes!*

Runs across the family room, down the hall, warp 9. Up the stairs, down the stairs, folds his legs and just slides down the carpeted stairway. Wild thing. Down the hall again, huffing and puffing all the way. Uses the futon for a flip turn. Oooooops, Peggy Sue was asleep on the futon. Now she's ticked off. She bellows at the intruder. This brings *(oh no!)* the Red Bitch out of the kennel she was napping in. Stiff-legged, hair on end.

Take-charge attitude. Earnie is trapped on the end of the futon. Peggy Sue is snarling at him, Becky is in his face. What to do? So over them he leaps and Rocket Man is off again! This time when he flies down the hall and through the door, Becky pins him. Classic, just like on TV. Gives him a couple of settle-down-Buster nose jabs. Everything returns to normal for the rest of the evening. Rocket Man is sleeping. The girls return to their naps. This scene will be repeated several times during the week. Love it.

Becky (Settle DOWN, ya little twerp, or I'll kick your ass into Friday!)
Peggy Sue (I'm getting a beauty nap here, get outa my face or I'll bite you where you like it the least!)
Earnie (Fast as fast can beeeeee! Betcha can't catch meeeeee! Wheeeee! Guys just gotta have fun!)

Michael & Scotty Richardson
The Golden Gang
Becky: The Red Scourge of Squirrels, Feline Track Coach
Peggy Sue: Pixie, Lover of Every Creature, Fecal Gourmet
Earnie: Marriage Test, Becky's Best Buddy, Chewin' Machine

HUNTING SEASON, DOGS?

As many of you on the list know, we spend a *lot* of time in the woods with our dogs. We hunt mushrooms, hike, etc., and the dogs accompany us. If we chose to leave them home because it's hunting season, they wouldn't be with us very often. There is almost no time when there isn't a hunting season of some sort going on out here in the NW. The Neanderthals are always shooting something. (Flame bait! Have at it!) Also prime mushroom hunting is during deer and elk seasons. While in the woods, we hang bells on the dogs (bear bells) and put blaze orange vests on them. No kidding. So far, so good. No shots have been fired our way. For the record, it's legal to shoot a dog for harassing wildlife out here. I guess if a hunter makes a mistake or purposely shoots a dog, he can always claim the dog was chasing deer. For this reason, I always carry a large caliber weapon, usually concealed. Yes, I have a permit. I believe I would be rather angry if my dog were shot for no reason. If the dog is harassing wildlife and gets shot, shame on me. If the dog is shot for no good reason, the shooter is going to suffer the consequences. This is called Darwinism.

Becky (You mean I could get shot for deer chasing?)
Peggy Sue (Yeah, but you can eat deer poop legally.)
Earnie (If I catch a deer, can I eat it?)

Michael & Scotty Richardson
The Golden Gang
Becky: The Red Scourge of Squirrels, Feline Track Coach
Peggy Sue: Pixie, Lover of Every Creature, Fecal Gourmet
Earnie: Marriage Test, Becky's Best Buddy, Chewin' Machine
Living in SW Washington State, USA

DO NOT SHOOT MY DOGS!

You can pay all the taxes you want. It won't stop someone from blowing your damn fool head off if you pull a gun on them. Just what the world needs, another Rambo Mushroom Hunter. "I carry a gun, and if anything happens, then they'll just have to pay." Give me a break. Is your big bad concealed gun bigger than your mouth in cyberspace?

Easy, big guy! There are anger management courses available, you know. Rambo? Nah. More like Woody Allen with a weapon. Scary, eh? If it would make you *feel better*, how about if we all carry our guns in the open? Sort of like Dirty Harry, big .44 or something? You *need* something to make you feel better. Take two aspirins and try again tomorrow—I love ya, man! People like you make me realize just why George Burns loved Gracie so much. It's *hard* to find a good straight man these days. Everybody wants to be the comedian.

Becky (So why is he upset?)
Peggy Sue (Yeah, doesn't he have goldens? He should act like them!)
Earnie (I love everybody! Particularly those with food!)

Michael & Scotty Richardson
The Golden Gang
Becky: The Red Scourge of Squirrels, Feline Track Coach
Peggy Sue: Pixie, Lover of Every Creature, Fecal Gourmet
Earnie: Marriage Test, Becky's Best Buddy, Chewin' Machine
Living in SW Washington State, USA

FECES CONTROL?

Sorry we missed a few postings, just got back from hiking the jungles of the Yucatan and found 800 messages awaiting us.

On the question of poop disposal, I will repeat last year's posting of my methodology. Of course, as most of you know, we are the proud owners of the *perfect* feces recycling system, none other than the Fecal Gourmet, Peggy Sue. Now, by running the feces deposited in your yard through an animal one more time (doesn't have to be a dog, BTW; mother-in-law, bad neighbor, anybody will do), you naturally end up with less bulk than if you only use the food once. Yes, of course, you will end up with some waste which must be dealt with. But you have reduced the size of the problem.

Just a suggestion. Now, the solution!

I tapped into the sewer clean-out just outside the house. Most homes on a city sewer will have an outside clean-out as well as most septic systems too. I extended a four-inch pipe up about two feet and installed a removable cap on it.

Whatever Peggy Sue doesn't eat goes into the pipe and into the city sewer system. You may also use this clean-out to dump your travel trailer tanks provided you use biodegradable chemicals in your tanks. This has worked well for us, no odors, no flies, no problems.

I have to admit I got a good chuckle out of all the suggestions to stop poop-eating. Oh yeah, tried 'em all. In most cases, a poop-eating dog is a poop-eating dog. All that *really* works is to follow the dog and clean up immediately. Or get some recipes for poop pies, feces pieces, etc., to give your dog some variety.

Becky (Oh no, not burm burrito time again, is it?)

Peggy Sue (Dad's dooley disposal really foils me, if I'm not quick!)
Earnie (Ah, geez, this is the *weirdest* damned family—)

Michael & Scotty Richardson
The Golden Gang
Becky: The Red Scourge of Squirrels, Feline Track Coach
Peggy Sue: Pixie, Lover of Every Creature, Fecal Gourmet
Earnie: Marriage Test, Becky's Best Buddy, Chewin' Machine
Living in SW Washington State, USA

MORE FECES CONTROL?

Jackson, our seven-month-old golden has started eating his own feces, and we don't know why or how to stop him.

Uh oh, sounds like a challenge for Peggy Sue!

Peggy Sue wishes to tell one and all she is in a class by herself. It's OK to compare your burrito biters to her, but she's the one, the *only* Fecal Gourmet. BTW, she really enjoyed the change when we used meat tenderizer on her yard yummies.

Becky (I'm a good dog, I don't get famous. Peggy Sue eats crap—she's world renowned! Something is wrong with the system. I think I'll vote Republican next time.)
Peggy Sue (Ha! You're jealous, red bitch! I told you, try it, you'll like it!)
Earnie (This has got to be a girl thing, right? Guys don't eat poop—do they?)

Michael & Scotty Richardson
The Golden Gang
Becky: The Red Scourge of Squirrels, Feline Track Coach
Peggy Sue: Pixie, Lover of Every Creature, Fecal Gourmet
Earnie: Marriage Test, Becky's Best Buddy, Chewin' Machine
Living in SW Washington State, USA

PLEASURE TEDDY?

Warning! Possible "R" rating!

Just had to tell the list how we are handling Earnie's uh, humping problem.

No, for *him* it's no problem. However, for Becky and The Pigger (and I don't like the way he's watching me) it's a problem. Caught all the solutions people provided concerning the "Humpmaster" last week. Saltpeter? Nah. We came up with a workable solution. At least we like it, we're not sure the Big Teddy likes it. Earnie, being six months now, has a *full load* of testosterone. Raging hormones. Rough play with the girls inevitably leads to humping! Now while this type of activity really doesn't bother human pack members around here, we haven't (yet) been on the receiving end (no pun intended) of Earnie's immoral maneuvers. Pity the poor girls! Peggy Sue, poor passive little creature, has been hassled ad nauseam. Becky gets really POed and grumpy. So we had to stop Earnie from buggering, er, bugging the girls. The command when we see the problem emerging is: NO HUMPING! in a huge voice. Now sometimes, if he's already started, he falls off the girls onto his side where he air-humps while winding down like a cheap watch. Usually, if we catch him in time, we tell him to "go get Hump-D-Bear. Hump-D-Bear (or Bugger Bear, never been sure) is a badly tattered, no nosed, one-eyed two-foot tall oversexed pleasure Teddy. He/she is all that remains of the woobies once roaming free around our home, until Earnie the Scourge killed 'em all, ate their guts, and ripped up the empty body shells. We figure this must be love. Strange relationship, this pup and the bear. Appears to be primarily a physical attraction. He never sends flowers or buys dinner and wine. Little foreplay. Sure he's good looking, but I should think the bear would reach its limit at some point. For the time being, the relationship works. Don't mess with success, right? ;-)

Becky (DADDDDDDDDD! Get this creep off me before I remodel his face!)
Peggy Sue (Why can't he have normal bad habits—like poop-eating?)
Earnie (Hey Beaaarrrrr! C'merrrreeeee Bearrrrr! I love youuuuuu!)
Hump-D-Bear (I have no idea how this relationship started. At least he didn't kill me.)

Michael & Scotty Richardson
The Golden Gang
Becky: The Red Scourge of Squirrels, Feline Track Coach
Peggy Sue: Pixie, Lover of Every Creature, Fecal Gourmet
Earnie: Marriage Test, Becky's Best Buddy, Chewin' Machine
Living in SW Washington State, USA

THE GREAT WHITE HUMPER

Earnie wishes to advise the list that as of now he is to be known as "The Great White Humper," and as you can see, we have changed our signature to comply with his wishes. We tried in vain to explain to him that he is a *hunting* dog. He insists that this is a misnomer, what the books actually should have said was *humping* dog. Whatever. He certainly takes pleasure from both activities. As I write this, he's at my feet abusing Hump-D-Bear.

All I can say is I don't know where he finds the energy for his amorous activities after a five- mile run today and a bath. We even show rinsed him so he'd smell good to his bear. Perhaps we should regard him as a role model. Beats the heck out of Dennis Rodman or Madonna. At least Earnie is true to Hump-D-Bear. So far.

Becky (Dad! I don't like the gleam in Earnie's eye!)
Peggy Sue (Oh no! The Fecal Gourmet and The Great White Humper in the same family!)
Earnie (You're jealous. At least I'm a famous lover, not a berm-burrito aficionado!)
Hump-D-Bear (No relief in sight—please, please, buy him that Speaker of the House doll!)

Michael & Scotty Richardson
The Golden Gang
Becky: The Red Scourge of Squirrels, Feline Track Coach
Peggy Sue: Pixie, Lover of Every Creature, Fecal Gourmet
Earnie: Marriage Test, Great White Humper
Living in SW Washington State, USA

HONEY, HE ATE IT

This morning while eating breakfast I dropped the "honey dipper" on the floor. It *had* a small, marble-sized wooden ball on one end that popped off and rolled across the floor. Before I had time to react, you guessed it—The Great White Humper, galloping gourmet, the dog who eats anything that hasn't eaten him first, old bucket-mouth—Earnie, our six-month-old golden had swallowed it. He certainly didn't have any time to chew, I had his mouth pried open and did a search-and-seizure routine within seconds, to no avail. We have had experience with dishrags, hand towels, pea gravel, bark dust, fir cones, etc. All the above items have passed through. Has anyone had experience with a small round object such as this? Should we just wait and see what comes out? This too shall pass? My gut feeling (no pun) is that he will pass it, as his turf-tacos are bigger in diameter than this object, but I am worried about it exiting the stomach. Advice?

Becky (My advice is to teach the little nipper not to eat everything he sees!)
Peggy Sue (My gourmet snacks are digestible, at least. What does he think he is? A beaver?)
Earnie (It was small, it rolled, it smelled like honey. What can I say?)

Michael & Scotty Richardson
The Golden Gang
Becky: The Red Scourge of Squirrels, Feline Track Coach
Peggy Sue: Pixie, Lover of Every Creature, Fecal Gourmet
Earnie: Marriage Test, Great White Humper
Living in SW Washington State, USA

THINGS THAT SUCK AND BLOW—

WARNING: The following has nothing to do with hips! Just another cute story. Delete now if you suffer an aversion to being amused!

The recent thread on vacuum cleaners prompted me to share this with the list. All our dogs react differently to air moving devices. Becky *loves* vacuums, air compressors, etc. If it sucks or blows, it's fun! If I fire up my twin air compressors (sometimes, we move a lot of air in this house, how's this for opening the door for you, pseudocomics), she's right there, insisting to be blown off at 120 psi. She cranes her neck, postures, makes sure I get her rump thoroughly. She also likes the big shop vacuum. This is one of those 7½ hp things that is guaranteed to suck a bowling ball through a chain-link fence. The above items are known as the "Hissing Hose Monsters" in this house. However, the pressure washer, commonly known as the "Hissing Pi**ing Hose Monster" scares Becky.

Peggy Sue doesn't care for vacuums or air hoses, but she thinks the Hissing

Pi**ing Hose Monster is a hoot. Water play at 3,000 psi. Needless to say, we don't let her near the darned thing for fear of grievous injury. She did manage to sneak around the corner while I was cleaning algae off the patio last summer though. She completely disappeared in a cloud of green slimy spray. My wife was not amused. Pigger got a bath and was kept in the house while the pressure washer was in use. I was told to wipe the smirk off my face.

Earnie doesn't have any love for the big upright Royal vacuum, but he isn't really afraid of it. But get the battery-powered hand-vac out of the closet, and he's outa the immediate area. Ah aren't they great?

Becky (Air hose alert! Get that itchy spot right behind my tail, dad! Ahhhh right there, that's it—)

Peggy Sue (Someday I'm gonna catch that Pi**ing Hose Monster. Wow! Look at the neato stream of water to chase!)

Earnie (You keep that dust-buster away from me and Hump-D-Bear!)

PSYCHO PIGGER?

The following may seem amusing, but at times it really isn't. Peggy Sue, now five years of age, has always been a total wuss. A sweetie pie. Cuddly fluff ball. Totally nonaggressive to the point of being timid. In the last month or so, she has decided to try and kill all the other dogs on the hiking trails we frequent. So far all confrontations have been on-lead, with no harm done except to my wife's arm which was stretched a few inches from

Pigger lunges. Earnie and Becky look at her with amazement, as they rarely react at all to other dogs, except a bit of normal sniffing. Even they appear shocked by her behavior.

What's going on here? Is she going nuts? It's really embarrassing for us to have this fifty-three-pound benign-looking cutie suddenly turn into something so out of character. It's like a Barbie Doll with fangs. A Chia pet with an attitude. Woody Allen with boxing gloves. Weird. Her attitude toward people hasn't changed. Still a lover. She has not been attacked by other dogs, we see no obvious reason for her to want to kick ass and take names. PMS? I doubt it, she's neutered. Any advice?

Becky (Hey I can handle myself. I don't need any blonde floozy protecting me!)

Earnie (I don't understand. I love everybody, that's why they call me the "Happy Humper!")

Peggy Sue (Let me at 'em! I'm gonna KICK SOME BUTT! Grrrrrr!)

Michael & Scotty Richardson
The Golden Gang
Becky: The Red Scourge of Squirrels, Feline Track Coach
Peggy Sue: Pixie, Lover of Every Creature, Fecal Gourmet
Earnie: Marriage Test, Great White Humper, aka Happy Humper
Living in SW Washington State, USA

CLOSET DRINKER?

I *really* wasn't going to admit this; call it a form of denial. Friends, I must come clean. We too have a closet drinker in our house. Water closet, that is. The primary reason I wasn't going to admit to this is because *neither* of the girls have ever sipped from the porcelain throne. Never been a problem before. Lowering the lid is something *no real man* should ever be forced to do. It's a guy thing; we leave the lid up simply because we *know* it irritates our wives and daughters. I *love* the sound a wife makes in the middle of the night when she discovers the hard way that the toilet seat was not lowered! For thirty-five years, I was the only male in the house. I left the lid up to remind the females in the house there was a man living here too! But now—along comes Earnie. Closet drinker. Great White Humper. A guy with a *real* drinking problem. After we rationed his drinking bowl, he located another source! A bottomless bowl! An endless fountain! Three bathrooms in this house and *all* the lids up! Imagine our surprise after we had rationed his water to watch him run to the door, ask out, and then three seconds later pee about three quarts on the dining room floor!
Arrgghhh! Where did he get that water? So Dawg Detective goes to work. We followed him. He's pretty sneaky, but we soon realized that he was going downstairs to drink from the thunderbucket where we couldn't hear his slurping noises. He wasn't too fussy about water quality, either, much to our dismay. Yuck! The outcome of this story is the women in the house won again. The lids are closed!

Becky (Mud puddles, rivers, streams, lakes—no toilets! Ugh!)
Peggy Sue (But of course, my dears, the yard is where I prefer to dine!)

Earnie (Slurpslurphumpthebearpeerunpoopdrinkhumphumpsleepzzz zzzzzzzzzzzzz)

Michael & Scotty Richardson The Golden Gang
Becky: The Red Scourge of Squirrels, Feline Track Coach
Peggy Sue; Pixie, Lover of Every Creature, Fecal Gourmet
Earnie: Marriage Test, Great White Humper, aka Happy Humper
Living in SW Washington State, USA

DOG SNOT, DARK WINDOWS

Some of you may have been on the list long enough to remember when we had to part with the beloved "Hairmobile," our 1980 VW Vanagon. World's best dog hauler. After it died a slow death with only three hundred thousand or so miles on it, we were forced to purchase a (gasp) new van. The criteria for purchasing the new car were simple. It had to please my wife (her car!) and had to be a practical dog hauler. After a few weeks of dealing with car salespeople, we were at the point of needing blood pressure medication when my wife decided on a new Plymouth Voyager. She liked the "sport" model which came with mag wheels, power everything—and those dark windows. First, allow me an opinion of putting mag wheels etc. on a van. Sort of like putting lipstick on a sow. A pig is a pig, a van is a van. I digress. My personal feelings on dark windows have always been that they usually hide the local drug dealer. Can't see in. If you look really hard, you might see the flash of gold chains and diamond rings on his person. I avoid these cars. Never, never, flip them the bird in traffic. You can't tell if they're reloading their guns behind that glass. But! Voila! There *is* a practical purpose for dark windows, I discovered accidentally! While washing the car the other day (not something we do often, BTW), I looked through the darkened windows at an angle—my God! *What* is on those windows? I opened the door and examined the inside of the windows. It looked like all the slugs and snails in the great NW had partied for the last month inside that van! From the outside, though, it looked *clean*! After thinking about it for a few moments, I realized that our new addition, Earnie, had been spending a lot of time in that backseat lately. Earnie has a nose about the size of the average steer. Up until now, I thought the favorite place for that humongous honker was in

Becky and Peggy Sue's crotches. Maybe not. Judging from the amount of slime on those windows, he may have found another honker heaven. Oh well, sometime this spring, we'll probably get around to washing the windows. In the meantime, we'll have to be judicious about who we take to dinner with us, anybody sitting in that backseat better be dog people!

Becky (If his nose is on the window, it isn't in MY CROTCH!)
Peggy Sue (Sliming the windows must be a guy thing, eh?)
Earnie (I can hardly wait until they wash the windows—this is a form of art!)

Michael & Scotty Richardson The Golden Gang
Becky: The Red Scourge of Squirrels, Feline Track Coach
Peggy Sue: Pixie, Lover of Every Creature, Fecal Gourmet
Earnie: Marriage Test, Great White Humper, aka Happy Humper
Living in SW Washington State, USA

PIMPCH COLLAR?

After being kept on pins and needles by the saga of "Harley Humpmaster, PhD," and longing for the magic cure, I must admit I was baffled by the use of a pinch collar to stop humping. I just don't see how this could work.

Then—it came to me! Just *what* portion of Harley's anatomy was the collar used on, anyway? Perhaps we don't want to know!

Becky (This is one time I'm really glad that gentlemen prefer blondes!)
Peggy Sue (If this keeps up, I'm going to the hair parlor for a dye job.)
Earnie (*WHERE* did he put that pinch collar? OOOOOooooo I bet that smarts!)

Michael & Scotty Richardson
The Golden Gang
Becky: The Red Scourge of Squirrels, Feline Track Coach
Peggy Sue: Pixie, Lover of Every Creature, Fecal Gourmet
Earnie: Marriage Test, Great White Humper, aka Happy Humper
Living in SW Washington State, USA

"YOUR" DOG, DAMMIT

Ever heard those word before? In this house, they're two of the most dreaded words imaginable, right up there with "that neighbor lady," "divorce," "fire," "wrecked car," "bounced check," etc. Yesterday, I heard those words. Scenario: Husband arises from bed, opens bedroom door, staggers bleary-eyed into hallway. Wife, early riser, lurking, yea, looming, at the end of hallway. Arms crossed. Eyebrows almost touching, *big scowl. Not* smiling. Uh oh. This doesn't look good. Times like this I'm always glad she never learned to use my handguns. Not a dog in sight, either. *Very* bad sign. There are *always* three pot-lickers wagging and thumping walls when I arise. Not this morning. Uh-oh. And then the dreaded words: "You'll never guess what *your* dog did this morning!" Uh oh. "So tell me honey, sugar, sweetie—what did he do?" says I. "You know those chairs we just spent $800.00 to have re-upholstered?" says wife. "Yeah, the green chairs, the ones that have been in your family for one hundred years, your favorite green chairs, right?" Says I. "Yes, *those* chairs! Just *look* at what *your* dog did to them!" I stumble into the living room. I spot the dogs, all peering intermittently around the corner of the dining room door. They are *not* coming any closer. They have their "oh, man, are we in trouble now" looks about them. I look at the chairs. "What's the problem?" I ask. "Look at the legs!" shouts wife. "Oh yeah, there used to be eight legs on the two chairs, right?" says I. Uh oh. Only seven legs. Better count again, it's early. Nope. Still seven. Hmmmmm. No need for Dawg Detective here. Obviously the work of The Great White Humper. Earnie the Beaver. Dang. How to placate this angry wife? Gotta think fast, too early for this stuff! I tell her "no sweat, I can fix it!" Knowing full well I have *no* idea how to do this. But it sounds good. I *do* have an idea though. Haven't shared this with my wife, so I'll run it by the list. How about I cut the other seven legs off so they all match? Sure the chairs will be only a foot high—sort of low-rider chairs. Might start a new fashion! Maybe tomorrow when my wife is gone I'll try that! Think it'll make her happy? Maybe I better order some flowers, just in case?

Becky (I *didn't* do that, I wasn't in the area, I wasn't even home—look at his eyes, dad. He's guilty!)
Peggy Sue (I'm outa here! Ass-kickin' time! I am not a crook!)
Earnie (What a place to live! No humping, no chair chewing, can't get on the furniture, why don't you just send me to military school! Anyway, I like your idea of cutting all those legs off. Then can I chew on 'em?)

Michael & Scotty Richardson
The Golden Gang
Becky: The Red Scourge of Squirrels, Feline Track Coach
Peggy Sue: Pixie, Lover of Every Creature, Fecal Gourmet
Earnie; Marriage Test, Great White Humper, aka Happy Humper
Living in SW Washington State, USA

DEADLY TENNIS BALLS?

Well, I don't know if the dyes in tennis balls are poisonous or not, but if they are, my dogs should have died (dyed?) fifty times over by now. This was a pretty average day, and Becky and gang did about forty long retrieves in the meadow. I get about three hundred feet distance with the tennis racquet, so they spend a *lot* of time with tennis balls in their mouths. Of course, there *are* rules. I don't allow them to suck on them. I also discourage them mixing their daiquiris with them. I figure the gin in their martinis kills anything on the tennis ball that replaces the olive though.

Becky (Those daiquiris are great after a long day in the field!)
Peggy Sue (A beer and a Berm burrito for me, please!)
Earnie (So you thought *I* had a drinking problem, eh?)

Michael & Scotty Richardson
The Golden Gang
Becky: The Red Scourge of Squirrels, Feline Track Coach
Peggy Sue: Pixie, Lover of Every Creature, Fecal Gourmet
Earnie: Marriage Test, Great White Humper, aka Happy Humper
Living in SW Washington State, USA

STRANGE LOOKS?

Your wife becomes angry when the pup chews off the leg of her favorite antique chair. You consider getting rid of the wife.

You arrive at the vacuum cleaner store with a dog-hair covered sample of your carpet and dare the sales person to find you a machine that will clean it.

Your friends arrive for dinner. Your pup commences humping his teddy bear.
You tell them to ignore him. They don't stay for dessert.

Michael & Scotty Richardson
The Golden Gang
Becky: The Red Scourge of Squirrels, Feline Track Coach
Peggy Sue: Pixie, Lover of Every Creature, Fecal Gourmet
Earnie: Marriage Test, Great White Humper, aka Happy Humper
Living in SW Washington State, USA

RESULTS, "YOUR DOG"

The ingenuity of those on this list never ceases to amaze me. I thought I would share a few of the snippets and suggestions I received after Earnie chewed on Michael's chair.

Cut the legs off all the furniture in the house. Only entertain people under five feet tall. Play a continuous recording of Randy Newman's "Short People Got No Reason to Live" on your stereo.

Defang the dog. Ha. The wife, maybe; the dog, *never!*

Spread nasty-tasting stuff all over the furniture we wish to keep. Peggy Sue likes it.

Call the doctor and have the wife "put down." Wife says, "If I go, the dog goes!" Took three days to get through to Dr. Kevorkian only to find he doesn't do dogs.

Becky (I only chew sticks I find in the yard. I like to make barkdust. I don't do chairs.)
Peggy Sue (Does this mean that Earnie stays? I wanted his toys.)
Earnie (Well, hey, it was a cherry-wood leg, and, like it was George Washington's birthday, and well I was just celebrating a bit. What's the big deal?)

Michael & Scotty Richardson
The Golden Gang
Becky: The Red Scourge of Squirrels, Feline Track Coach
Peggy Sue: Pixie, Lover of Every Creature, Fecal Gourmet
Earnie: Marriage Test, Great White Humper, aka Happy Humper
Living in SW Washington State, USA

BEARNERIAL DISEASE?

Arrgghhh! Earnie has developed an infection in a very private area. We suspect this may be "related" (pun) to Hump-D-Bear in some way. Our vet says it's just a simple "sheath infection" easily treated with saline solution and Panalog. Hmmmm. I think I'll take Earnie and Hump-D-Bear down to the free clinic and get 'em checked anyway. At least, Hump-D-Bear gets a bath! Oh this is just toooooo gross! Now I know what you breeders go through—I can't believe what the treatment for this entails.

Becky (Serves him right! Keep him away from us girls, OK? Or I'll whip his little humpty butt!)
Peggy Sue (See, at least my bad habits don't cost any money.)
Earnie (Geez, Dad, I bet you never thought your fingers would be in *that* place. More Panalog, please, that feels good!)

Michael & Scotty Richardson
The Golden Gang
Becky: The Red Scourge of Squirrels, Feline Track Coach
Peggy Sue: Pixie, Lover of Every Creature, Fecal Gourmet
Earnie: Marriage Test, Great White Humper, aka Happy Humper
Living in SW Washington State, USA

BEWARE HEAT REGISTERS

This morning one of the things we learned about on this list and thought would never happen to us—happened. Brought the "kids" back from our daily walk and fetch, grabbed a glass of water, and sat down at this computer. Usually I remember to remove collars when the dogs are in the house. Old-timer's disease struck this a.m. and I forgot. Shouldn't have been a big deal, right? Wrong. Earnie was warm from the exercise and laid down on the heat register for the breeze, something he does regularly. Next thing I know he is running frantically out of the room running into walls, doors, and ki-yi-ing as if the devil himself was after him. I ran him down in the hallway to find that his tags had slipped through the heat register, and it was hanging from his neck. He released his anal glands all over the computer room, piddled all the way down the hall, mmmmmm smells sooooo good in here! Poor little guy was really frightened. I hate to think of what might have happened had I not been here when this happened. I guess this is a good reminder to all of you: *remove those collars when you are not with your dogs!*

Becky (What the—? Hey, Earnie, is that a new piece of jewelry? Cool!) Peggy Sue (I'm outa here! Whatever is after Earnie is gonna get me too!) Earnie (Oh, man, I thought I was dead. Did you see the look in the eyes of that malevolent register when it grabbed my neck? Thanks, Dad, for saving me. Sorry about the smell :-(!)

Michael & Scotty Richardson
The Golden Gang
Becky: The Red Scourge of Squirrels, Feline Track Coach
Peggy Sue: Pixie, Lover of Every Creature, Fecal Gourmet
Earnie: Marriage Test, Great White Humper, aka Happy Humper
Living in SW Washington State, USA

HOLLYWOOD? HUH?

Golden listers:

I've got an idea which will make Michael and Scotty rich beyond their dreams. A new TV sitcom entitled, *Life with Earnie!* Can't you see it? A couple with a wonderful sense of humor and a new, exasperating golden retriever puppy named Earnie.

I could do the rich part. Perhaps get Earnie a gold collar. Earrings. Lip studs. Tattoos. Sport coat for Hump-D-Bear. Perhaps a jeweled chastity belt too. For Hump-D-Bear, of course. The biggest hurdle I see to the success of this plan would be the new rating system on TV. I doubt much of what Earnie does that's interesting could be aired to the general public.
Although, I'm sure we could tone down the racy parts (keep Hump-D-Bear partially clothed, etc.) to assume a PG rating.
One problem with your above statement—the part about the "couple" with a wonderful sense of humor. Some of what Earnie does (actually, MOST of what he does!) is not amusing as far as my wife is concerned. Typical woman, doesn't understand about "guy" stuff, male bonding, etc. For instance, she was not amused about the chewed chair leg and was somewhat disgusted when Earnie accomplished his mission with Hump-D-Bear the other night. Total disbelief. Disgusted. Repulsed. Hey it's a guy thing. Anyway, we're up for fame and fortune. Bring it on!

Earnie (Hey, Peggy Sue, know what's oversexed and underloved and hums?)
Peggy Sue (No, what?)

Earnie (Hhhuuummmmmmmmm!)
Becky (You're disgusting! Hey, Dad, how 'bout taking him back to the breeder?

Michael & Scotty Richardson
The Golden Gang
Becky: The Red Scourge of Squirrels, Feline Track Coach
Peggy Sue: Pixie, Lover of Every Creature, Fecal Gourmet
Earnie: Marriage Test, Great White Humper, aka Happy Humper
Living in SW Washington State, USA

TOUGH GOLDENS—HA!

Does anyone have a good comment for when someone does something to your dog that you don't approve of? Since I'm not confrontational, it would have to be something *nice* but that gets the point across.

I always said "careful! She's guard-trained!" with our Doberman? (And my wife!) Perhaps we could try this with our goldens? No? Don't think it'll work? I dunno, Earnie looks pretty tough (VBG)! I bet *nobody* will fool with him after we get the spiked collar and do some well-placed body piercing. Nose ring, stud between the eyes? Hey it works for me. I *never* say much to the punk rockers I see on the street, do you?

Earnie (Fight? Bite? You *must* be kidding here!)
Becky (Don't mess with the redhead!)
Peggy Sue (Fifty-three pounds of rompin' stompin' candy ass!)

Michael & Scotty Richardson
The Golden Gang
Becky: The Red Scourge of Squirrels, Feline Track Coach
Peggy Sue: Pixie, Lover of Every Creature, Fecal Gourmet
Earnie: Marriage Test, Great White Humper, aka Happy Humper
Living in SW Washington State, USA

FRONTAL NUDITY?

Scotty Richardson wrote:

Frontal nudity may be a problem. Hump-D-Bear has neuticles.

I have a problem with this. First, we have confirmed that Earnie is a boy, right? Now you say that Hump-D-Bear has neuticles, which may mean that Hump-D-Bear used to be a boy? And you are permitting this relation to continue? (VBG) Or is Hump-D-Bear a female trying to act tough for Earnie?

Since inquiring minds want to know, you may recall in an earlier post that we were unsure of Hump-D-Bears sexual orientation, as well as the gender. In the interest of sex education, a couple of neuticles and a foot of garden hose have created an anatomically correct Bear. Sort of the Long John Holmes of the bear world. "B" movie fodder. Or "X" if you prefer. Of course, we could be dead wrong; perhaps Hump-D-Bear was a girl all along in which case this is sort of embarrassing (pun) for all involved. Perhaps I should quit while I'm ahead. If I am ahead.

Michael & Scotty Richardson
The Golden Gang
Becky: The Red Scourge of Squirrels, Feline Track Coach
Peggy Sue: Pixie, Lover of Every Creature, Fecal Gourmet
Earnie: Marriage Test, Great White Humper, aka Happy Humper
Living in SW Washington State, USA

EARNIE AND THE MOVIES

Ever try to sit down and play a movie all the way through without interruptions? Do you have an eight-month-old pup? Does it work? Arrggghhh! In our house, this is how it goes: rent movie, take the golden kids on the ride to video store. They like this part. Come home, take all the dogs out to potty. Empty those bladders well! Poop if necessary. OK. Back in the house. Chew bones all around. Settled in, right? Pop the Laserdisc into the player. Hit play. The disc begins to wind up. So does Earnie. I swear he uses the whining of the laser player as his cue for mischief. The rest of the movie goes like this: Earnie finds three tennis balls. Jams them all into his mouth. Looks like he has a terrible disease, bad case of the mumps. Earnie drops tennis balls in front of recliner chair. Earnie shoves them under recliner chair. Earnie begins trying to dig them out. Carpets won't take this kind of abuse. Scotty yells "no digging!" Earnie goes out to hallway. Finds three more balls. Shoves these under the futon. Tries to dig them out. Pause the movie here. Wife on hands and knees with yardstick, getting balls out from under the furniture. Earnie helping, head under the futon, butt in the air. Quite a sight. OK, hit play. Earnie finds all the balls, repeats the stuffing them under furniture act. Pause the movie. Dig out the balls. After three or four of these ball-jamming exercises, movie watchers get frustrated. Time to put peanut butter in the Kong! Earnie carries Kong to kitchen, drops it on the floor and looks up expectantly. Scotty fills Kong with peanut butter. Back downstairs. Hit the play button. Enjoy fifteen minutes of movie except for the loud sucking and slurping noises created by Earnie sucking peanut butter out of Kong. Earnie finishes peanut butter, stuffs Kong under chair. Starts digging again. Scotty has about had it by now—yells "OK, knock it off!" Earnie stops digging and shoving balls under furniture. Now he has to pee. Take dog out. Dog pees. Dog sniffs the yard interminably. Back in the house. Can't get away with the ball stuffing thing anymore, so hassles and humps Peggy Sue. Scotty yells "no humping!" Earnie winds down with frustrated look on face. Replay the above, over and over. The movie was 131 minutes. It takes four hours. Oh well. Naturally, when the movie ends, pup goes to sleep. So do pup's owners.

Earnie (Oh boy, a movie! Stuff fetch dig pee gotta go out, here hey, hey, gotta go out!)
Becky (I'll just nap behind the chair where the whirling dervish can't get to me.)
Peggy Sue (I just KNOW he's gonna get bored and try to hump me! I'm gonna give him *such* a bite!)

Michael & Scotty Richardson
The Golden Gang
Becky: The Red Scourge of Squirrels, Feline Track Coach
Peggy Sue: Pixie, Lover of Every Creature, Fecal Gourmet
Earnie: Marriage Test, Great White Humper, aka Happy Humper
Living in SW Washington State, USA

WATER-SHY GOLDENS?

Hello to everybody, this is my first contact in this list, and I'm glad to get the possibility to ask if somebody can give some tips to get a water-shy golden in deep water that he starts swimming.

Becky, our rescue dog was a bit over a year old when she came to live with us. She had been cooped up in a back yard, slept either outside or in a garage. Never been named. Never seen a lake or river. She was terrified of the small waves along the beaches of the Columbia River where we first introduced her to water. It took months of coaxing her to follow me while I waded into increasingly deeper water, tempting her with a stick or tennis ball thrown *just a few feet* farther out into the river all the time. Finally, she just took off swimming with a "geez, look what I've been missing" look on her face. At the ripe old age of two, she followed me off a twelve-foot cliff into a swimming hole in a nearby stream. Sploosh! Big cannonball, doggy style! I think you just have to work up to the deep water part slowly and patiently. Be cautious not to frighten the dog. Once they start swimming, your biggest problem will be how to keep them out of the water. Count your blessings; many is the time my dogs have gotten into really slimy snotty stuff and required much bathing before entering our house!

Becky (I'll swim in anything, if it's wet! I like to leap off high places into the water with dad! I swim in the heavy surf in the Pacific Ocean!) Peggy Sue (I do the swimming part, but I leave the leaping stuff to the insane red dog. I'm a lady.)

Earnie (I'm not swimming yet, but I've been in up to my chest! Soon, soon. Summer is coming and there will be tennis balls to fetch out of the river!)

Michael & Scotty Richardson
The Golden Gang
Becky: The Red Scourge of Squirrels, Feline Track Coach
Peggy Sue: Pixie, Lover of Every Creature, Fecal Gourmet
Earnie: Marriage Test, Great White Humper, aka Happy Humper
Living in SW Washington State, USA

DON'T EAT YELLOW GRASS

Gosh, I hate to be a scofflaw here, but the posts about female neutered dogs whose urine doesn't kill the grass must have been written by the folks who believe in the Easter Bunny, the Good Fairy, etc. Ha! Unless you run Scotts Lawn Fertilizer through your spayed bitches, you *will* have a polka-dot lawn! Last time I checked, it's a bad practice to add lawn fertilizer to your dogs' diet, so don't do it. Anyway, what's your objection to yellow spots in the grass? Breaks up the monotony of all that booorrrinnnggg beautiful green turf. I find the yellow areas don't grow as fast and require less mowing too. If you have enough dogs, all your grass will die, allowing you to spend the weekend on holiday enjoying yourself instead of doing drudge work in the yard. Lawnmowers are a major contributor to air pollution, and dog piss isn't. Kill all your grass and clean up the air! Of course, if you simply cannot deal with the yellow spots, there *is* a simple solution. Wait until dark and potty your dogs on the neighbor's lawn. When they complain that something is killing their grass, wave your arms, gesticulate wildly, and mutter about a government conspiracy. Wear camo clothes and clean your assault rifles in sight of the neighbors. Yellow grass will become the least of their worries, and you will be left alone with your pristine lawn. It works for me.

Becky (Yeah, I leave yellow spots, but so does Dad when we all go out for final potty.)
Peggy Sue (I only pee in one corner of the yard, so *al** that grass is dead!)
Earnie (Hey I pee all over and don't kill the grass! So to compensate, I eat clumps of it and dig a bit! Gotta keep up with the girls!)

Michael & Scotty Richardson
The Golden Gang
Becky: The Red Scourge of Squirrels, Feline Track Coach
Peggy Sue: Pixie, Lover of Every Creature, Fecal Gourmet
Earnie: Marriage Test, Great White Humper, aka Happy Humper
Living in SW Washington State, USA

EARNIE—A STAR?

OK, everybody who thought Earnie should be on TV, instead of just rolling tennis balls under it, listen up! I called the Neuticle Man for some information (no, they're not for me) and a couple of bumper stickers. A surprise for my wife's van. I wonder if she'll like them. Anyway, the Neuticle Man wants a dog for national TV ads. Here's the deal—if we neuter Earnie, he gets on TV! We didn't think about this one too hard, as

the breeder wants to show him. I'm afraid with her medical background, I just might be the next candidate needing neuticles.

Earnie (Me? Famous? You're gonna tutor me on TV?)
Becky (I think it's a great idea! I'll toss in a month supply of my chew bones if you neuter the little runt!)
Peggy Sue (No more humping? NO MORE HUMPING? All right! I'll kick in some of my treats too!)
Hump-D-Bear (How do I spell relief? N-E-U-T-E-R! Would he quit eating my face off?)

Michael & Scotty Richardson
The Golden Gang
Becky: The Red Scourge of Squirrels, Feline Track Coach
Peggy Sue: Pixie, Lover of Every Creature, Fecal Gourmet
Earnie; Marriage Test, Great White Humper, aka Happy Humper
Living in SW Washington State, USA

EARNIE VS. THE RED BITCH

Today, it happened. While I was whacking tennis balls into the fields for the dogs to retrieve, Earnie got the bright idea of challenging Becky, alpha bitch, sixty pounds of muscle, retriever extraordinaire, for a ball. Mistake. Off they go, Red Bitch in the lead, seven-month-old, seventy-pound Earnie, aka "Bubba," gaining on her slightly, galloping along at her flank. At top speed, they both dive for the ball. Picture rolling bodies, fur flying, grass in the air. Up they come. Becky has the ball, and a smirk (I swear!) on her face. Earnie has a sore leg and the wind knocked out of him. Scared me at first, he stood there and snapped at his left hind leg like there was a bee on it. I rushed over and checked him out, no apparent problem with the leg. After a bit of hobbling around, he proceeded to chase balls again with no sign of discomfort. But, he didn't challenge the Red Rocket again. Peggy Sue, always the lady, just watched from a distance. Smart dog, Peggy Sue!

Becky (I told ya and I told ya—don't mess with me, or I'll kick your pretty-boy butt into the next county! Old age and treachery outdo youth and vigor every time!)
Peggy Sue (Egad! I think I'll stay in the other half of the pasture. Too rough for me! Maybe I can find something interesting to roll in!)
Earnie (Whoooooffff! Whew! Anybody get the number of that truck? Oooooo that smarts! I'll try again tomorrow! Maybe tonight I can sneak up and hump her!)

Michael & Scotty Richardson
The Golden Gang
Becky: The Red Scourge of Squirrels, Feline Track Coach
Peggy Sue: Pixie, Lover of Every Creature, Fecal Gourmet
Earnie: Marriage Test, Great White Humper, aka Happy Humper
Living in SW Washington State, USA

DEAD HUMP-D-BEAR?

Did I miss something? When did Earnie KILL HDB? Was there a funeral? Was he cremated? I'm so sad! :-(

Ditto! Scotty . . . is THAT why you've been so "silent?" Please, you can tell us what happened! Where should flowers or donations be sent? (I can't wait for an answer to this one!) Is Earnie "handling" it OK? Was it a suicide? I can't believe Earnie would do that . . . intentionally.

It was a crime of passion. I doubt Earnie meant it, it happened in the heat of the moment. Perhaps Hump-D-Bear said something that irritated him, like "no" or "not tonight, I have a headache." We may never know. We discovered the remains of Hump-D-Bear one morning, the whole face, eyes, nose, and all, gone. Just gone. We have kept the remains, it could be that the poor bear is not beyond resurrection. Easter is upon us. We are all keeping watch. He/she may rise again, who knows? Perhaps when we are through babysitting the grandson for the next couple of weeks, and Michael has time to do major surgery we may yet save the bear. We will keep the list posted.

Becky (Fix the bear! Maybe that'll keep the brat from hassling me all the time. My head is a slobbery mess. Danged drooley Earnster, anyhow!)
Peggy Sue (Will he keep that size ten nose out of my crotch if the bear is repaired?)
Earnie (OOOOOooooo I miss my buddy. Is there a chance the bear will return?)

Michael & Scotty Richardson

The Golden Gang
Becky: The Red Scourge of Squirrels, Feline Track Coach
Peggy Sue: Pixie, Lover of Every Creature, Fecal Gourmet
Earnie: Marriage Test, Great White Humper, aka Happy Humper
Living in SW Washington State, USA

POOP-EATING DOG?

I spotted the posts claiming that feeding the "natural" diets causes poop-eaters to abstain from turf-taco tippling. I think we will have to say that is true. Since we changed to the Pitcairn diet several months ago, Peggy Sue, aka The Fecal Gourmet, inveterate turd eater, Burm Burrito specialist, Poopsicle lover has apparently stopped eating her stools. This may be temporary, but we are encouraged. This is the first time in her five years that she has shown a lack of interest in her poop. Perhaps we're on to something here?

Becky (Her breath is better!)
Peggy Sue (The new food tastes better fresh than recycled. It's that simple!)
Earnie (I still can't believe anybody would eat dog poop. Bird poop, horse poop, cat poop. Maybe.)

Michael & Scotty Richardson
The Golden Gang
Becky: The Red Scourge of Squirrels, Feline Track Coach
Peggy Sue: Pixie, Lover of Every Creature, Fecal Gourmet
Earnie: Marriage Test, Great White Humper, aka Happy Humper
Living in SW Washington State, USA

WHAT DOGS SAY

Last night while walking our dogs on the trail, a large mixed breed dog came bounding over the hill at us while its owner screamed "COME!" at it to no avail. It marched right up to my dogs and sniffed noses. It looked like everything was going to be OK until Peggy Sue said something. I listened closely to the conversation between the four dogs, and I'm sure I understood most of what was said. Probably my remarkable ability to translate what they were saying was at least partly due to the fact that I recently read The *Secret Lives of Dogs* by Elizabeth Marshall Thomas. Now, I don't claim to be a literary critic, but aside from my learning dog language from this book, the only other thing I gleaned from it was the fact that if this woman and her dogs lived next door to me, there would surely be a homicide. If I let my dogs run the way she does, I would expect
Animal Control on a daily basis.
Anyway, what I think Peggy Sue said was "you're ugly, your mother dresses you funny, and she sleeps under the porch." The other dog responded with "yeah, and your father is a son-of-a-bitch!" At this point, Becky stepped in and told the strange dog that not only was he ugly, he smelled bad, and he was dumber than a box of donut holes. Earnie was standing by taking all this in, when the other dog decided he was going to kick Peggy Sue's cute little ass. Peggy Sue said "just try it! My little brother can whip you good!" At this point, the trash talk stopped and the action began. Michael ran the strange dog off with a tennis racquet, thereby saving the day and probably Earnie's good looks. A pox on all people who allow their untrained dogs to run off lead. Listen closely next time your dogs get into it—I bet you too can understand "The Secret Language of Dogs."

Peggy Sue (I think Earnie coulda took him!)
Becky (If he couldn't, I KNOW I could!)
Earnie (Damn, I hate big sisters. Their talkin' trash is gonna be the end of me yet!)

EARNIE—WATER DOG?

Yesterday it happened! At the ripe old age of nine and a half months, Earnie has become a water dog! We took Earnie and the girls out in our canoe for a couple of hours. Earnie's first canoe trip. Interesting, to say the least. Becky is an excellent boater; she will stay dead center in the canoe and not flop around. I can tell her which way to move to trim the boat, and she understands. Peggy Sue sits in front of Michael in the bow of the canoe, where she can be controlled. She wants to lean over and snap at the waves—very disconcerting in rough water. Earnie sat in between my knees in the stern, where I could keep the ornery little sucker from flopping around like an injured trout. He was having lots of fun but had no idea he could tip us over. After an hour of continually sitting him down he settled in. Upon reaching shore, I grabbed the tennis racquet and started hitting balls out into the lake. Earnie dove in after a ball and looked a bit surprised when his feet left the bottom. He'd never been in swimming before. At first his butt sank, and he floundered around, I wasn't sure I wouldn't have to go in after him—but he soon paddled with his back feet and off he went! He retrieved balls with the girls for two hours and didn't want to get in the truck to go home! Today, we took them back to the lake and hit balls into the water—Earnie is now a faster swimmer than Peggy Sue and can almost stay with Becky. Amazing how quickly they learn. When they're ready to swim, they swim. We never rushed him, he just decided it looked like fun, and in he went. Today, there were large waves breaking on the shore—he thought those were a hoot—he got knocked down a few times, but it didn't seem to frighten him. Guess he's ready for summer fun!

Becky (I can still out swim him—but I can't carry two balls like he does! Ball hog!)

Peggy Sue (Now there are TWO danged idjut dawgs competing with me for those tennis balls! Dang! Good thing Dad hits them right to me, or I'd never get one!)

Earnie (Wow! Now I know why that Alpha Red Bitch likes the water so much!

Hit the ball! Hit the ball!)

Michael & Scotty Richardson
The Golden Gang
Becky: The Red Scourge of Squirrels, Feline Track Coach
Peggy Sue: Pixie, Lover of Every Creature, Fecal Gourmet
Earnie: Marriage Test, Great White Humper, aka Happy Humper
Living in SW Washington State, USA

FINALLY GOT ONE

Big day today for Becky. After three years of living in this squirrel-infested area—she got one! Our yard is fenced, so it's generally fairly simple for the squirrels to dart under or over the chain link. Today, with a little help from Earnie—she managed to corner one. Now for those of you who think like my wife horrified at the idea of *killer* dogs, think about this: we have three dogs. They average three times a day at least, going out into the yard. So to keep this simple, that makes around three thousand trips into the yard in three years. Each time they go out—there are several sassy, smart-aleck squirrels who sit in the tree and taunt them. Becky has probably chased squirrels out of her yard over one thousand times. Been close, got one by the tail once—but it got away. Put yourself in her place. How frustrating. Sort of like deer hunting for years with no luck. Like fishing for days without a bite. So today, there was no hesitation or was there anything I could do to stop it. She was all over that little sucker like a cheap suit. One little killer headshake—dead squirrel. She tossed it in the air, and Earnie caught it. Michael was horrified. We did take the furry critter away from them. I worry more about fleas and disease than anything else. Becky and Earnie looked very proud of themselves. After all, they *are* hunting dogs!

Becky (GOT ONE! GOT ONE! Hahahahahahahahahah damn I thought I'd never get one man this feels good!)
Peggy Sue (Oh this is too gross! I just sit and watch them. I cannot believe you two killed that poor little critter!)
Earnie (Too cool, Becky! Now I know what a squirrel tastes like! Mmmmmmgood! Let's go after another one, hey?)

Michael & Scotty Richardson
The Golden Gang
Becky: The Red Scourge of Squirrels, Feline Track Coach
Peggy Sue: Pixie, Lover of Every Creature, Fecal Gourmet
Earnie: Marriage Test, Great White Humper, aka Happy Humper
Living in SW Washington State, USA

TENNIS BALL TERRORIST?

Anybody else have this problem? Earnie, our sweet-natured, loveable, slow-moving, ten-month-old golden boy gets totally weird when he has a tennis ball. He changes from lover-boy to the *Tennis Ball Terrorist*! He pushes it under the furniture and tries to dig it out, no matter how many times you tell him to knock it off. He dips the dang things in the water bowl. He then pushes the wet, slimy thing into your lap (or anybody's lap that's handy) running snot trails (pupkus?) up your pants. This is a real wake-up call if you're wearing shorts. If that doesn't get your attention, he'll slime your bare arms and hands. Once he managed to put one in my bare armpit. That got my attention. Arrggghhh! Yeah, I know, take the tennis balls away, right? We have tennis balls in every drawer, on every tabletop, shelf, kitchen counter, and anyplace else we figure he can't reach them. He always manages to find one—I swear they just appear; perhaps they really are breeding under the bed. In the next couple of days, I plan to check all the tennis balls for gender. The males will go to the lake and be drowned. Think this'll work?

Becky (First, he killed all the woobies. Now there aren't any tennis balls to play with because of him! What's next?)
Peggy Sue (Hey, Dad, is it too late to take him back to the breeder?)
Earnie (I've got a ball, hey see, I've got a ball! Pay attention now, or I'll snot your arm! Throw the ball, throw the ball!)

Michael & Scotty Richardson
The Golden Gang
Becky: The Red Scourge of Squirrels, Feline Track Coach
Peggy Sue: Pixie, Lover of Every Creature, Fecal Gourmet
Earnie: Marriage Test, Great White Humper, aka Happy Humper
Living in SW Washington State, USA

MR. BUTTERBALLS

Sometimes being a male isn't all it's cracked up to be. Consider the following: Yesterday, took the fur kids up the mountain to hunt some 'shrooms. They aren't very good at hunting 'shrooms, but they excel at squirrels, deer, elk, and of course, the ever-popular leavings of the above creatures. The girls are old hands at this mushroom stuff. Experienced woodsmen, er, ladies, so to speak. Earnie, on the other hand, at ten months, still has much to learn. Today, he learned a valuable lesson. The forest is full of pitch right now, and it's normal to clean pitch off the feet, feathers, etc. of the girls. Butter, real butter, does the trick. Rub it on the pitch; they lick it off along with the pitch. Now males have a problem that females don't. Certain portions of the anatomy of males hangs a bit lower than the females. Out here in the great NW, some of the downed trees are fairly large, four feet or so in diameter. Anything under two feet is considered brush for you Easterners. So you have to jump *high* from time to time to clear the logs. Apparently, Earnie didn't jump *quite* high enough on an occasion or two. We noticed a lot of licking going on during the ride home in his, er, belly area. Upon closer examination here at home, we found his testicles to be quite covered with pitch. His licking only made matters worse. What are we going to do? I asked my ever-so-wise wife. "What do you mean 'we'?" was the reply I got. "You got a mouse in your pocket?" she asked. "He's YOUR dog!" said she. So I got out the butter and told Earnie to roll over. Dang, he liked it. I think the next time the stubborn little sucker won't come in when I call him all I need to do is yell "Hey, Earnie! Want your balls buttered?" I bet he comes a-running!

Becky (Why is he smiling like that?)

Peggy Sue (I dunno, but I don't think he's got gas—)
Earnie (Rub it in, rub it in, rub that butter on my skin, oooohhhh
yeahhhh!
Eat your heart out, Christopher!)

Michael & Scotty Richardson
The Golden Gang
Becky: The Red Scourge of Squirrels, Feline Track Coach
Peggy Sue: Pixie, Lover of Every Creature, Fecal Gourmet
Earnie: Marriage Test, Great White Humper, aka Happy Humper
Living in SW Washington State, USA

WE'VE BEEN SLIMED

Before we made the final decision some ten months ago to bring Earnie, our
golden boy, home, we thought we had heard *all* the reasons not to have
a male dog. "They are oversexed and will hump the chairs, the other
dogs, the neighbor's cat, the neighbor, etc. etc." OK, we can deal with
that. "They tend to be aggressive if not neutered, and will fight other
dogs, etc. etc." OK, we can deal with that. "They smell like a musk ox,
and they leave little pecker-tracks wherever they lay." OK, what are a
few pecker-tracks between friends? As far as the odors go, well I know
people who smell worse than my dogs. At least I can bathe the dogs. Try
giving a foul-smelling friend a bath sometime. What we were *not* told
was: They have loose lips. Not the kind that sink ships. The big, floppy,
jowled kind that hold a quart of water after the dog takes a drink, and
then dribble it *all* over the floor fifteen feet around the drinking bowl.
Earnie leaves enough water on the kitchen floor that OSHA has declared
it an unsafe walking zone. If it were just water, it probably wouldn't be so
slick. But once water has entered his mouth, it becomes—slime. What
dribbles on the floor could be used as a lubricant for auto engines. It's
similar to wallpaper paste. Except stickier. You could use it in place of
Scotchguard—nothing sticks to it, and it sticks to everything. Earnie
goes into the next room and you hear this "flapping" sound, similar to a
flock of geese rising off a pond—he's shaking his head. So what? I'll tell
you so what! When he shakes his head, long slimy strings of lugubrious
dog saliva go every direction, sticking to the ceiling, the walls, the floor,
the furniture—and *you,* if you happen to be within thirty feet of him.
When it dries, it leaves trails of sparkly stuff like old slug or snail trails.
Did you see *Ghostbusters?* Remember the scene where the ghost "slimed"

Bill Murray? That's what happens when Earnie shakes his floppy jowls! So—if you're in the area and you want to pick Michael or I out of a crowd—look for the slime trails! That's us!

Peggy Sue (If you think that's bad—look what he does to the water bowl when he drinks! It looks like somebody poured clear gelatin in it! Yuk!) Becky (Hey wrestle with him. My whole body gets slick and slimy! He bites me on the face and all my fur is matted together. Icky-poo!) Earnie (Why are you all running away from me? I was just gonna shake my head a bit!)

Michael & Scotty Richardson
The Golden Gang
Becky: The Red Scourge of Squirrels, Feline Track Coach
Peggy Sue: Pixie, Lover of Every Creature, Fecal Gourmet
Earnie; Marriage Test, Great White Humper, aka Happy Humper
Living in SW Washington State, USA

EXPENSIVE TASTES?

"My son," as he is becoming known around the house, has done it again. I'm sure there are those on the list who remember Earnie eating a leg (only one!) off my wife's newly upholstered antique chair. That was several months ago. Until yesterday, damage has been minimal since that chair episode. A few minor items chewed, a few divots in the lawn, and in the last several months, only one small piddle in the house. On with the story. Michael and I had to be gone all day yesterday, flew to Idaho, and picked up a new truck. Left early. My buddy came over and fed and pottied the dogs, and spent some time playing with them. Not as if they were abandoned. Earnie and I have been going to obedience school the last three weeks. I have been with him every day, twice a day, doing his "lessons." Not a latch-key dog. Lives in the house with us and Becky and Peggy Sue. Never alone. Until yesterday. Seems as how his idea of letting us know he wasn't happy with getting left was to eat the arm off the over-expensive futon downstairs. My wife *had* to have this thing, cost $900.00. As far as I'm concerned a futon is an uncomfortable couch that makes into an uncomfortable bed. I don't care what they cost. They're crap. But why, oh why, with all the junk furniture in the house did he have to eat the futon? Perhaps it has something to do with the fact that it used to be a very important portion of his route whenever he had the FRAPs (frenetic rapid activity period, FWIW). The futon was used for a flip turn, much as a swimmer makes a flip turn at the end of a pool. I repaired the darn futon once already, seems as how even expensive futons don't withstand sixty-five-pound dogs using them for flip turns. Had to reglue all the joints after it literally fell apart. Or maybe he just knew I don't like the thing and decided to do me a favor and eat it. Only Earnie knows for sure. What I know for sure is that "my son" and I are in the doghouse!

Becky (I TOLD him not to do that! I even offered a chew bone!)
Peggy Sue (Hey! That's my favorite bed spot! Don't be chewing that futon up!)
Earnie (Well, I was bored, and you left me all alone, and I didn't even get my lesson, so what did you expect? Hey! That TV looks real tasty—!)

Michael & Scotty Richardson
The Golden Gang
Becky: The Red Scourge of Squirrels, Feline Track Coach
Peggy Sue: Pixie, Lover of Every Creature, Fecal Gourmet
Earnie: Marriage Test, Great White Humper, aka Happy Humper
Living in SW Washington State, USA

NATURAL DIETS—THE TROTS?

OK, we have a problem here. Earnie has spent the last two nights panting and moaning at the foot of our bed. In my younger days, panting and moaning in the bedroom were good signs. Now it just keeps me awake and causes my wife to sleep in the other room. Earnie appeared to be too warm or in some other discomfort. Experience has taught me not to panic and run to the vet every time something like this comes up. If we did, we might as well have a live-in vet. Anyway, the day before yesterday, Earnie started with loose stools, which now are full-blown diarrhea. You know, the variety where you can poop through a screen door and never touch the mesh? Still, no panic, out with the Pepto-Bismol and wait twenty-four hours until panic time. Then last night, Peggy Sue developed really *runny* poop too. Now Peggy Sue has *much* longer feathers than Earnie, and the only way to clean her up is with the garden hose. Yech! These are *house dogs!* This morning, Becky got it too! Now, we panicked. Off to the vet for a triple prescription of Metronidazole, a medication which our dogs are on quite a lot, usually due to "beaver fever" they pick up from the marsh below the house, or from eating grass which was covered in water during the flooding this spring. This time, we know that could not have caused this. The dogs have not been in the meadow for a week or so. We fear that the raw meat we have been feeding on this modified Pitcairn diet may be the culprit. Has anyone else out there had this problem? We have been feeding this diet for six months now, with excellent results. This is the first big problem. All three dogs as I write this are lying about, listless, after having been medicated this morning. For now, the diarrhea has stopped or is under control. Thank God for small favors, eh? Naturally, this is the week we are sitting our two-year-old grandson. Naturally, he is attracted to the runny piles in the backyard. Hey this stuff is so runny you can't scoop it. You just turn on the lawn sprinklers and let it soak in. OK, enough descriptions already! Any advice? Should we try cooking the meat? Or is this just a coincidence of some kind?

Becky (OOhhhhhh my tummy hurts! But I sure would like some of that popcorn!)
Peggy Sue (I hope this clears up soon. I'm tired of getting my butt hosed off. I didn't ask for a bidet, hey?)
Earnie (Sorry about the panting and moaning. Maybe tonight we can all get some rest. Do you suppose this has anything to do with the futon I ate?)

Michael & Scotty Richardson
The Golden Gang
Becky: The Red Scourge of Squirrels, Feline Track Coach
Peggy Sue: Pixie, Lover of Every Creature, Fecal Gourmet
Earnie: Marriage Test, Great White Humper, aka Happy Humper
Living in SW Washington State, USA

POOP-SOUP CURED?

OK, out there, I know you were holding your collective breath on this issue!

After only one dose of Flagyl, the trots are gone! We will continue (at the vet's advice) the pills for seven days. Our vet is so used to these dogs getting giardia from the water around here that his office just makes up the medication with no appointment needed. Normally, as in this case, Flagyl puts a quick halt to the runs. Earnie has spent the entire morning romping in the sprinklers with our two-year-old grandson, so I guess he feels OK. The other two furkids have regained their perky dispositions and will once again come to the sound of potato chips being opened from anywhere in the house. All is well! Thanks to all of you for your help. Great list, eh?

Earnie (Whoaaaaa. I'm sure glad that's over. I sure got tired of running in and out.)

Becky (I'm surprised you even *went* out, you nasty little pup!)

Peggy Sue (Hey I kinda liked it. Poop soup! Over the teeth, 'cross the gums—look out tummy, here it comes!)

Michael & Scotty Richardson
The Golden Gang
Becky: The Red Scourge of Squirrels, Feline Track Coach
Peggy Sue: Pixie, Lover of Every Creature, Fecal Gourmet
Earnie: Marriage Test, Great White Humper, aka Happy Humper
Living in SW Washington State, USA

GOLDEN TRICKS?

Since Windsor is now one year old, I must say how impressed not only of his intelligence but the willingness to learn and accomplish new doggie "tricks."

I'm curious to know what other goldens out there know how to perform those outstanding tricks.

One favorite of Earnie's is to balance a ball, preferably a tennis ball, of course, on his nose. He will stare cross-eyed at it until I tell him to "get it" at which point he flips it off his nose and catches it in his mouth. This is an easy trick for Earnie, I admit. His head is the size of a basketball (but much harder), and the muzzle stop where his nose meets his forehead would hold a large cup of tea. My girls have more trouble keeping the ball balanced 'cause their noses aren't as wide as your average buffalo.

Becky (Just let him try that trick while I'm around! I snatch the ball right off the little sucker's forehead!)
Peggy Sue (Yeah, that really cheeses him off too!)
Earnie (Jealous bitches! Grrrrr!)

POOR MAN'S PEACHES?

Out here in the great NW, we refer to the large banana slugs as "poor man's peaches." Ever eaten canned peaches? Slime city. Enough said. About the only creatures I know of except the French (sorry!) that will dine on these gastropods are ducks and geese. If you are attempting to rid yourself of the slugs/snails inhabiting your flower beds without using poisons, you could just turn a few geese loose on your property. However, if you are a golden retriever owner, as most of us on this list are, there is a strong possibility that mixing your goldens with geese or ducks could be trouble.

Perhaps, Denise of Mallard Manor would care to comment on this. In the meantime, I think I'll entertain myself by going out in the yard with a salt shaker and turn over some rocks.

Becky (Slugs! Yuk! You mean geese eat them? I'll never hunt geese again!)

Peggy Sue (Well, do slugs taste anything like poop? Perhaps I've found a new food source here!)

Earnie (I sort of envy them. They're the only creatures alive that can leave a bigger slime trail than I can. Dog snot only goes so far!)

Michael & Scotty Richardson
The Golden Gang
Becky: The Red Scourge of Squirrels, Feline Track Coach
Peggy Sue: Pixie, Lover of Every Creature, Fecal Gourmet
Earnie: Marriage Test, Great White Humper, aka Happy Humper
Living in SW Washington State, USA

POOOOOOOOP?

Peggy Sue (aka Fecal Gourmet) has proven to us that *nothing* short of cleaning the yard immediately or offing the dog will cure this problem. She is a connoisseur, only consumes her *own* waste. We changed our dogs to a modified Pitcairn diet several months ago, and it appeared for a bit that she had stopped eating her turf tacos. Wrong. It just took an adjustment period for her to realize that poop is still good, even if it's natural poop with no preservatives. She *knows* we really think her habit is disgusting, there is no guiltier look on earth than Peggy Sue caught in the act of burm burrito consumption. She will actually spit it out if caught and try to smile, or perhaps a s***- eating grin would better describe her facial expression. I should clear up another point here— even though she won't eat another dog's feces, she has no problem with eating human, deer, elk, cat, duck, goose, sparrow, or the poop from any other creature that walks, crawls, or flies. Hey we tried all the "cures." Jalapeno, red peppers, she just thinks she's eating Mexican that night. Adolph's meat tenderizer adds zest! Canned spinach makes her strong like Popeye! The commercial stuff you buy at the wholesalers only pique her interest! So if you have a poop-eater, you probably either clean up your yard or learn to live with rectum breath. Pigger-kisses can be very revolting from time to time. No worse than kissing a smoker, I guess. Ah well, we love her and perhaps she's just being tidy and cleaning up the yard, eh? ;-)

Becky (Disgusting—just really disgusting. But the deer, elk, etc. is really good stuff!)
Peggy Sue (Hey, Dad, don't knock what you haven't tried! Wanna kiss?)
Earnie (This has gotta be a girl thing. I just can't believe this. Yech!)

Michael & Scotty Richardson
The Golden Gang
Becky: The Red Scourge of Squirrels, Feline Track Coach
Peggy Sue: Pixie, Lover of Every Creature, Fecal Gourmet
Earnie: Marriage Test, Great White Humper, aka Happy Humper
Living in SW Washington State, USA

OF ALL THE THINGS
TO CHEW ON

Do you think we could train Levi to destroy the couch in the family room but not the replacement? We are looking for an excuse to change the colors in that room.

Best regards,
John

Dear John: I doubt training will be necessary. Levi is related to Earnie, I believe. Earnie was delivered to us with full knowledge of how to destroy furniture. It's instinctive, I'm sure. Bred in. Thanks a lot, Sue and Norma!
Patience, John, Levi is young yet. He hasn't even gotten the finer points of carpet-staining down yet, has he? Earnie didn't move on to furniture until he was five or six months old. We think he likes the taste of varnish. If you need any pointers on woobie killing, humping, and furniture-wrecking, we are here for you. Trust us. We're here to help.

Becky (Maybe Earnie could go live with Levi, sort of a live-in trainer?)
Peggy Sue (I'll buy the airline ticket.)
Earnie (Nobody understands me. I ain't had no fun since Hump-D-Bear died. Hey Levi, need some help?)

Michael & Scotty Richardson
The Golden Gang
Becky: The Red Scourge of Squirrels, Feline Track Coach
Peggy Sue: Pixie, Lover of Every Creature, Fecal Gourmet
Earnie: Marriage Test, Great White Humper, aka Happy Humper
Living in SW Washington State, USA

POOR MAN'S—PEACHES? UGH—

In a message dated 97-07-21 18:24:03 EDT, couver@pacifier.com (Scotty
Richardson) writes:

*Out here in the great NW we refer to the large banana slugs as "poor man's
peaches."*

*They have slugs here that look like hamsters (no, I'm not drinking). They
are the same size and color . . . Yuck!*

*A few weeks ago, they had a warning here about these slugs and dogs. It
seems that they carry some kind of worm that will kill dogs if not treated.*
Great . . . something else I have to keep out of her mouth ;-)

Well, let me say this about that—*hamsters!* I hope you're kidding; if
not, where do you live so we can avoid going near there? I cannot
imagine even the least discriminating dog (even Peggy Sue) putting a
slug in their mouths though. My dogs have eaten some pretty disgusting
stuff—but so far, no slugs! BTW, have you written to Stephen King
about these hamster/gastropods? I'm pretty sure there's a great horror
story here somewhere.

Peggy Sue (Yeah well, you say poop-eating is disgusting—but I saw you
eat raw, slimy oysters! Now *that's* gross!)
Becky (Yeah, and how about celery? That stuff really sucks and you
eat it!)
Earnie (Are these hamsters/slugs big enough to hump? Hmmmm.)

Michael & Scotty Richardson
The Golden Gang
Becky: The Red Scourge of Squirrels, Feline Track Coach
Peggy Sue: Pixie, Lover of Every Creature, Fecal Gourmet
Earnie: Marriage Test, Great White Humper, aka Happy Humper
Living in SW Washington State, USA

EARNIE'S FIRST BIRTHDAY!

Thursday is the Earnster's first birthday! I'd like to say it seems like only yesterday he was just a little nipper—but that might stretch the truth a bit. If you read my posts, you *know* I would never do that. Gee it's great to sit and reminisce, savoring his golden moments of puppyhood! I'll never forget the first few weeks, trying to keep Becky from killing him. The pensive, "take him back" looks from Peggy Sue—and from my ever-patient wife, from time to time. The yellow puddles on the white kitchen floor—ah, yes, I remember it well. Of course, after he got a little older and was allowed out of the kitchen, there were the spots on the carpet. If you looked at the carpet in just the right light, you could pick out designs. Like Rorschach tests. Right from the start, Earnie was a creative pup. As he grew, so did his creativity! Who could forget that morning I awakened and walked down the hallway listening to my wife yelling: "You'll *never* guess what *your* dog did this morning!" Hey; so he ate the leg off her antique chair, nobody is perfect, right? It was obvious from the start Earnie had certain tastes. Drapes, bedspread fringes, throw rugs, and, of course, hardwood furniture were all to his liking! A true connoisseur! I remember his first few outing to the forests too! He was attempting to eat every rock, dirt clod, fir cone, or anything else we were too slow to pry out of his jaws. Too cute! How about my lawn? I can hardly believe the divots he's eaten out of it. Some of them have yet to grow back, poignant reminders of his youth and Earnthusiasm! To this day, he never ceases to amaze us! I'm certain he holds all records for woobicide; he never met a stuffed toy he couldn't destroy in under a minute! I will admit that Hump-D-Bear was an exception, perhaps because Hump-D-Bear was the only stuffed toy he ever met who didn't say "no!" to his, er, sexual advances! Alas, Hump-D-Bear eventually died too, perhaps as a result of too passionate lovemaking. We'll never be sure; we just found poor Hump-D one morning, no eyes, no ears, no nose, no stuffing. Dead. Gone to the Happy Humping Ground. Probably the direct result of a headache. Just when you think Earnie's all grown up, he does something to remind you he's a pup yet. Like getting the FRAPs nightly. Wild forays about the house or yard! Flip turns off the futon! Ricocheting off the walls! Hey you always know when he's around! To celebrate his own birthday, last night he really outdid himself! Just as we were falling asleep with all three dogs in the bedroom, we heard the dreaded "up-chuck-upchuck-upchuck" sound. Out of bed I flew, hoping to at least get a towel under Earnie, who was attempting a world-record target vomiting episode in the center of the wall-to-wall carpet. Didn't make it. As I stood there, two and a half cups of slightly digested, warm dog food rolling across my toes, I knew we wouldn't have missed having this first year with him for anything. John, if you're reading this, look at all you have to look forward to!

Becky (If Ida killed him the first week you wouldn't be standing in a puddle of puke right now—)
Peggy Sue (Hey is that stuff still good to eat?)
Earnie (Well, there went dinner. What's for breakfast? Do I get birthday cake?)

Michael & Scotty Richardson
The Golden Gang
Becky: The Red Scourge of Squirrels, Feline Track Coach
Peggy Sue: Pixie, Lover of Every Creature, Fecal Gourmet
Earnie: Marriage Test, Great White Humper, aka Happy Humper
Living in SW Washington State, USA

COME? WHO, ME?

In addition to these excellent suggestions, working on other commands and behaviors has been most helpful. Levi learned "come" in about three minutes yesterday, and we are all pretty excited.

Dear John: In regards to Levi learning "come" so easily, don't worry. This is indeed an anomaly. He'll get over this. Earnie did the same thing at that early age, but by the time he became *really* mobile, he unlearned the command for the next several months. He derived great pleasure from sniffing and marking while tuning out me calling him. This is commonly called "hard of listening" and all puppies go through this. Some, like Peggy Sue, become permanently, selectively "hard of listening." ("I can't heeeaaarrrrr you, Dad—") Fortunately, obedience school has taught Earnie how to hear again. Poor Peggy Sue, on the other hand, can only hear certain words and noises. For instance, she cannot hear "come" but has no trouble with "cookie" or the crinkling sound of a potato chip bag being opened three rooms away. Just pray little Levi doesn't turn out to be handicapped like Peggy Sue.

Becky (I think it's a blonde thing. I never had any trouble.)
Peggy Sue (Are you calling moi? I thought I heard something?)
Earnie (Holy cow! That trainer at school got really gnarly when I failed to come! It's easier to just come, I *hate* it when Dad has to come and get me!)

Michael & Scotty Richardson
The Golden Gang

Becky: The Red Scourge of Squirrels, Feline Track Coach
Peggy Sue: Pixie, Lover of Every Creature, Fecal Gourmet
Earnie; Marriage Test, Great White Humper, aka Happy Humper
Living in SW Washington State, USA

DOGS SMARTER THAN BROTHERS? HMMMMMM

John asked a good question the other day: Is it possible that Levi, his new golden pup isn't smarter than his brothers? Having pondered this question for a day or so, I believe I can cast some light upon this subject. For I also have two younger brothers, and am owned by three goldens, one of whom is male. Why does gender make a difference you ask? Is my bias showing? Perhaps. Females are smarter than males. Dogs, humans, whatever. Same thing. Girls are smarter. Ask my wife or my daughter. No arguing this one. If Levi were female, there would be no question, I could say with certainty that Levi is smarter than Johns's brothers. Touchy subject, this. One must remember that if we have brothers, that means we *are* one too! Over the years, my dog trainers have insisted that one *should* be smarter than the dog to train it. Now I'm older and wiser. I get it! They were trying to tell me something. All the trainers have been—female! Interesting phenomena, yes? Now, I'm about to admit something that's difficult for me. Earnie is beautiful, charming, fun, sweet, loveable—but there's a good possibility he isn't the "brightest light in the harbor," if you know what I mean. He's got a loooooong way to go to catch up to Becky, our wily red bitch in the smarts department. Perhaps he's just in a slower learning curve?

The original question remains: Are our dogs smarter than our brothers. OK, I'll offer a few scenarios, *all true*, and let you, the reader decide!

1. I never met a golden who snorted his entire estate and all his earnings up his nose for short-term pleasure. Sure goldens may eat a bit of poop now and then, nobody's perfect. Advantage: golden!
2. My younger brother used to fling himself off the back porch screaming "Scotty pushed me" when my folks weren't looking.

He would then scuttle about in a circle like a one-legged crab; howling in mock distress. My folks (knowing I was capable of such a thing) were fooled several times—resulting in me getting whomped upside the head or being taken to the woodshed. So far, Earnie hasn't proven to be a very good actor. His guilt is obvious when he's caught eating furniture or creating chaos with my lawn. Advantage: brother!

3. I have never seen a golden get drunk and make a total fool of himself. For the record, both my brothers and myself are guilty of this a hundred times over! Of course, some of us aren't too far from the "fool" department anyhow. Advantage: golden!

4. I have never observed my brothers eating the legs off the furniture or ingesting rocks, etc., causing them to become ill. I have seen my brothers overindulge in alcohol or overeat chocolate ice cream and get on a fairground ride causing general panic in the people below the ride, running to avoid a rain of vomit. Advantage: none!

I have never worried about Earnie getting AIDS, as he seems to practice safe sex with the furniture and pillows. Both my brothers, on the other hand—? 'Nuff said! Advantage: golden!

So, John, take this for what it's worth and make up your own mind. At least your brothers are interesting. I wish mine had nine-foot birds and fire trucks. Be sure to remember—we're brothers too.

Becky (You FINALLY admitted it! Earnie ain't the sharpest blade in the drawer, right? Red dogs are smarter than blondes. It's genetic.)
Peggy Sue (Are we into picking on blondes? You were doing OK after you admitted girls are smarter than boys—so don't push your luck!)
Earnie (I bet you think that just because I tried to swim upstream the other day where the water was too fast, I'm dumb! Hey, I was just working out! You didn't have to jump in and save me like that!)

Michael & Scotty Richardson
The Golden Gang
Becky: The Red Scourge of Squirrels, Feline Track Coach
Peggy Sue: Pixie, Lover of Every Creature, Fecal Gourmet
Earnie: Marriage Test, Great White Humper, aka Happy Humper
Living in SW Washington State, USA

PIGGER'S SKIN PROBLEMS?

After several years of fighting recurring skin problems, and at the advice of our vet, we finally took Peggy Sue to the doggie dermatologist in Portland, Oregon. Seems as how she has a (very) stubborn staph infection. In the past, we have treated her (at our vet's advice) with tar-sulfur baths, benzoyl-peroxide baths, and usually a couple of weeks of cephalexin, an antibiotic. The dermatologist basically is telling us to continue this treatment, except up the baths to (gasp!) once daily for fifteen minutes with a sulfur-based shampoo, then rinse that off and bathe for another fifteen minutes with benzoyl-peroxide. Along with this, nineteen days on the antibiotics, as well as a short course (three days) of steroids, methylprednisone. We are to bathe daily for three to four days, and then every other day for a couple of weeks and slowly decrease the bathing until the problem clears up. His advice is to always bathe at least once a week as a preventative measure with the medicated shampoos. OK, that's all well and good. But (get ready) because she has such a heavy coat, and because getting air to the skin helps these recurrent infections, he is recommending a field cut. I have seen people on this list get ballistic about cutting a golden's coat for the summer months. I admit we are at our wit's end with these skin problems having tried everything we (and our vet) can think of. So unless I see some good reasons not to—Peggy Sue (and maybe Becky) are getting summer haircuts. This dermatologist has heard all the stories about fooling with a

golden's "thermostat" and says there is no problem with a summer haircut, as a matter of fact, he thinks it's beneficial to dogs as active as ours. They dry faster after swimming and are much easier to get the burrs and grass seeds out of. Guess what I'm looking for here is anybody s experience with these "haircuts." Perhaps we will get Peggy Sue a Mohawk.

Becky (I'm a redhead—perhaps a "do" like Sarah Ferguson?)
Peggy Sue (A Mow hawk? Or a Mohawk? Too cool!)
Earnie (Stay away from me with those clippers! I like this long hair! How else am I gonna shed all over the place?)

Michael & Scotty Richardson
The Golden Gang
Becky: The Red Scourge of Squirrels, Feline Track Coach
Peggy Sue: Pixie, Lover of Every Creature, Fecal Gourmet
Earnie: Marriage Test, Great White Humper, aka Happy Humper
Living in SW Washington State, USA

LOVEY WITH A SKUNK?

Levi's favorite, though, is Ms. Skunk. In fact, Levi has been smitten by Ms. Skunk and has already begun amorous advances (and he's not even nine weeks old yet).

Dear John: My wife spotted this post and wanted you to know that it may not be a good idea encouraging Levi to make whoopee with a skunk. Metaphorically speaking, many of us may be guilty of just that, but then, we're only humans. Another story, another time—(VBG)!

Becky (Skunk? Peee—UUUUUUU! Why not buy Levi a stuffed dog?)
Peggy Sue (Yeah well, you guy shouldn't talk. Remember Earnie and that stoopid Hump-D-Bear? Gad, that was obnoxious!)
Earnie (Hump-D-Bear? Did someone mention that name? Oh how I loved that little bear. Too bad it got a headache and I had to kill it.)

Michael & Scotty Richardson
The Golden Gang
Becky: The Red Scourge of Squirrels, Feline Track Coach
Peggy Sue: Pixie, Lover of Every Creature, Fecal Gourmet
Earnie: Marriage Test, Great White Humper, aka Happy Humper
Living in SW Washington State, USA

THE GIRLS' NEW "DO'S"?

OK, guys, it's over—the girls are sporting new "field cuts," thanks to the doggie dermatologist. When we went to pick them up, the groomer was still working on Becky. Peggy Sue got clipped and kenneled before Becky saw her.

When Peggy Sue came bopping out of the kennel with her new "do," Becky got pretty weird. She did the toe-strutting walk all around Peggy Sue as if to say "who the hell are YOU!" Poor Peggy Sue. She looks like a large Chihuahua! Becky, on the other hand, has a marvelous figure and looks really good with short hair—sort of like a German Shorthair. If they were humans, Peggy Sue would resemble Bette Davis, and Becky would look like Jamie Lee Curtis! Both dogs still have about one-half their tail feathers, so they can still wag convincingly. The rest of their bodies have about three-fourths inch of hair left. They look a bit strange to us—sure hope this helps the skin problems.

Thanks for all of the private posts (over forty); your opinions really helped. It did become clear to us that many of you on the list are "closet clippers" as your dogs sport summer haircuts too. Guess you don't like admitting it on the list, eh? In answer to the holistic approach—yeah, tried that too, Richard, but thanks. Becky would be OK using that approach, but not Peggy Sue. BTW, this is only the second time in six years we have resorted to steroids, and remember, this is only a three-day course. Nothing to get anal about, IMHO. I don't approve of steroids either, but I have had to use them from time to time when nothing else worked. I have received private information on some other possible treatments too controversial to post to the list. If this haircut/cortisone/anti-biotic/bath thing doesn't do it, we will most likely try some of these. For now, I will miss all the dust buffalos crossing the kitchen floor. Two out of three dogs getting shaved should cut the shedding. Perhaps Earnie can shed more to help the girls out?

Peggy Sue (Hey! Becky! It's meeeeeee, dammit! Go ahead, sniff me! It's meee, I tell ya!)
Becky (Pigger? Is that *you*! I'll be danged? Are ya sure? You look too weird!)
Earnie (Oboy! Strange stuff! Lickdroolhumplickdroolhump)

Michael & Scotty Richardson
The Golden Gang
Becky: The Red Scourge of Squirrels, Feline Track Coach
Peggy Sue: Pixie, Lover of Every Creature, Fecal Gourmet
Earnie: Marriage Test, Great White Humper, aka Happy Humper
Living in SW Washington State, USA

HAUNTED VIRUS?

Hi Scotty and list:
A couple of years ago I worked for the BLM. When you work for the federal government, they feel the need to warn you about everything. This is not necessarily a bad thing, but anyway, one of the warnings we received was about deer mice being one of the carriers of the hantavirus which killed several people in New Mexico.

Hey didn't mean to get everybody excited about the hantavirus. Yeah, we know about it, and yeah, there are documented cases of it in Washington State. For the record, though, in both cases of "finding" deer mice nests, I had no warning they were there. The dirty little beggars failed to post any warning signs. OSHA and the FDA have formed an alliance to better educate these mice. They will be required to post little signs warning of their whereabouts. Failure to do so will result in citations issued by a neighborhood cat. Please don't worry any more about me getting hantavirus. I didn't inhale. Hey where have I heard that line before? As far as worrying about Becky catching something from a mouse, I feel compelled to remind you fellow listers of some of the *really* disgusting stuff our goldens, Becky included, carry about in their mouths. I doubt mousie-dung (pun) is a problem. Well, gotta go. It's time for me to sit on the deck and worry about being struck by lightning!

Becky (You mean those mice are dirty? How come the coyotes eat 'em, then?)
Peggy Sue (Hey compared to my "tastes" mice are considered germ-free! I wonder if they taste like poop?)

Earnie (Hantavirus attacks the respiratory system. Don't worry about Dad. He could suck a bowling ball through a chain-link fence!)

Michael & Scotty Richardson
The Golden Gang
Becky: The Red Scourge of Squirrels, Feline Track Coach
Peggy Sue: Pixie, Lover of Every Creature, Fecal Gourmet
Earnie: Marriage Test, Great White Humper, aka Happy Humper
Living in SW Washington State, USA

EARNIE HAS BEEN TUTORED

My precious golden boy is home from the doctor's office—all properly "tutored"! He's pretty sore and somewhat wobbly from the anesthesia. By tomorrow, he'll be feeling a lot better. His gait is noticeably affected—no more of the big side-to-side sway. He probably is about, oh eight or ten pounds lighter. Christopher would be proud!

Peggy Sue (Oh, thank god! I bet my back will get better now!)
Becky (Hey, Earnie, look at the bright side. You won't have clearance problems when you jump over logs anymore!)
Earnie (Geez I feel a lot lighter in the hind quarters? Does this mean I won't be missing Hump-D-Bear anymore?)

Michael & Scotty Richardson
The Golden Gang
Becky: The Red Scourge of Squirrels, Feline Track Coach
Peggy Sue: Pixie, Lover of Every Creature, Fecal Gourmet
Earnie: Marriage Test, former Great White Humper
Living in SW Washington State, USA

IT'S A GUY THING

The other night after bringing Earnie home from the vet's office minus his gonads, I got into an interesting discussion with my wife. Poor little Earnie was sitting funny (wouldn't you?) still somewhat affected by the recent anesthesia, eyes like pee-holes in a snowbank. My wife looked at me and said, "You look depressed."

"I am," I replied. "Why?" she asked. "Because I hated doing that to Earnie," I said. "Hmmmph!" said she. "It didn't bother you when we neutered the girls!"

"That's different," I said. "Why is it different?" she replied. "Because it just is, I don't expect you to understand, being female and all," said I.

At this point she glared at me and started making little piggy noises, her ever-so-subtle means of telling me I'm being a male chauvinist hawg again. This, of course, furthered my depression. I'm sure the men on this list know what I mean—the sucking sensation in the pit of our tummies when we think about being "tutored."

Earnie, during this discussion, was sitting at my feet, alternately puking from the anesthesia and trying to lick what was missing. I think he heard the whole discussion though. The next morning, he refused to leave the bedroom until I did. He would not eat food offered by my wife; I had to feed him. (Yes, this is true!) He blames her! I sure hope he never finds out I tried negotiating with the vet for a transplant. I figured I could have lots of fun with a fresh new set. The vet, ever a practical man, warned me against this transplant, claiming I would spend a lot of time chasing cars and urinating on tires. I'm not sure how he knows this, but I plan to keep a closer eye on him when I have Becky or Peggy Sue in his office.

Becky (I always thought there was a funny glint in that vets eye!)
Peggy Sue (Typical redhead. You think everybody is attracted to you! Blondes are beautiful—watch me strut!)
Earnie (Hey, what's the deal? Something's missing here! Dad! What did Mom do to me!)

THE MEANDERING BALL

On the way home from the Portland area G&H picnic yesterday, Michael spotted a yard sale. Being addicted to yard sales, she begged me to stop. We were looking for toys and books for our grandson, when Michael spotted a plastic ball, about four inches in diameter, with an electrical switch on it. "What does this ball do?" Michael asked the lady in charge. "It plays music if you put a new battery in it," she replied. The price was ten cents. Such a deal. We brought it home, took it apart, and put a new battery in it, to discover it didn't play music. It's one of those balls that rolls all over when you turn it on and reverses direction if it hits something. Acts like it's alive. Hmmmm. Possibilities here! After dinner, we took all three dogs down into the family room and turned on the ball. I haven't laughed so hard since the pigs ate my brothers! Earnie couldn't figure the thing out; he swatted at it and pounced like a cat—it rolled down the hallway, Earnie in pursuit. It hit the wall. It turned around and charged him! Earnie did a quick U-turn and retreated down the hallway! Halfway down the hall, his courage returned, and he turned on the ball, which was still chasing him, and proceeded to try and bark it to death! Becky and Peggy Sue were tired from a full day at the G&H picnic, having chased many a tennis ball. They were trying to sleep. All the ruckus coming from Earnie made that impossible. Finally, Becky got up, strolled up to the meandering ball, picked it up, and took it over and lay herself down on it. The look of disdain she gave Earnie said it all. Poor Earnie still steers clear of the killer ball!

Becky (Earnie, you dummy! It's just a mechanical ball, you doobus! You nutless, er, gutless wonder!)

Peggy Sue (What are you worried about, Earn? It's not like it's gonna bite your jewels off anymore—heeheeheeheehhee!)

Earnie (Look at its face! It's gonna get me, I tell you! This just isn't my weekend. First, I become a eunuch, and now that things trying to get me! Daaaaad!)

Michael & Scotty Richardson
The Golden Gang
Becky: The Red Scourge of Squirrels, Feline Track Coach
Peggy Sue: Pixie, Lover of Every Creature, Fecal Gourmet
Earnie: Marriage Test, former Great White Humper
Living in SW Washington State, USA

A VERY FETCHING REDHEAD

Woke up in a good mood today (for a change), decided to celebrate something. Back in my drinking days, I always found some reason to celebrate. More difficult finding stuff when you're sober. What to celebrate came to me when I was swatting tennis balls in the meadow for our three golden "kids" today! I figure we have been in this home for over three years. We average five days a week on our four-mile walks. Of course, that always includes off-lead time in the fields to hit *many* balls for the fur babies! On an average day, seven years *young* Becky (aka Air Dog) will do twenty-five fetches before she's ready to vomit. Peggy Sue, ever the demure lady, will fetch two or three balls and then roll on one for a while. Much less energy expended. Not in the "fetch 'til you barf" league. Earnie, being young and full of energy, usually runs between Becky and The Pigger trying to swipe a ball or two, with limited success. Sometimes stealing balls from the Wily Red Bitch can be dangerous as he has learned. However, Earnie gets more daily mileage than either of the girls. Typical guy—lots of chasing, not much catching. Anyway, I figured Becky does an average of twenty-five long fetches a day (as far as I can hit a tennis ball with a racquet) or 125 fetches a week, so that means that in a bit over three years the fetchometer has rolled over the 20,000 mark! Extemporaneous water-fetching, sticks tossed down canyons during mushroom hunts, etc., are not included in the numbers, so 20,000 is probably on the low side. Yes! A celebration!
Cake! Ice cream! Dog cookies! Junk food! Hmmmm. Becky is napping through the celebration though, as are Pigger and The Earnster. Party poopers! Well, perhaps tomorrow we'll celebrate by fetching a few balls. Guess I'll go read my book.

Becky (Hitthe ballhitthe ball! ARFARFARF! Gotta fetch the ball!)
Peggy Sue (Hey why so anal over a few tennis balls? Try rolling on one. It feels good, and it makes Dad nuts when you won't bring it back!)
Earnie (Puffpuffpuffpuffpantchase! Will somebody put a drag chute on that gnarly Red Bitch? Dad! She threatened me! I want a ballllllllllllll!)

Michael & Scotty Richardson
The Golden Gang
Becky: The Red Scourge of Squirrels, Feline Track Coach
Peggy Sue: Pixie, Lover of Every Creature, Fecal Gourmet
Earnie: Marriage Test, former Great White Humper
Living in SW Washington State, USA

THE FAMILY JOWLS

Nope, this isn't about Earnie's recent loss of his manhood. I spelled it right. Jowls. As those of you who have met Earnie know, he has a magnificent head. Mostly empty, admittedly. But large. His headgear includes a really phenomenal set of jowls. I'm not sure in liquid measure of their capacity, but judging from the vicinity of the water dish after he drinks, it looks like several gallons.

Yesterday after a rousing hour or two of fetching tennis balls on the meadow, I was returning up the trail with my furkids when a group of teenaged students on a walkathon suffered the misfortune of learning about Earnie's jowls. OK normally, when your dog isn't running or breathing hard, the saliva in the jowls resembles clear liquid. Sure when they shake their heads in the hall it leaves little shiny snot-stringers all over the walls. We're all used to that. But take one dog, exercise the dog hard, and that liquid saliva turns to foam! It also increases in bulk measure depending on how long and how hard you ran the dog. So up the trail toward my three foamed-up dogs comes about a dozen teen-aged girls squealing things like "oh aren't they precious?" As they bent to pet the dogs, I tried to warn them about the slime—they didn't seem concerned.

And then! Earnie leaned his head slightly to the left, as if there was something in his ear. Me, the savvy owner, immediately moved to the far end of the six-foot leash. He leaned his head to the right. To the left again, gaining velocity. Then he shook his head with a loud "FLAPPA-WHAPPA-FLAPPA" sound, similar to sheets blowing in the wind on a breezy day. Like playing cards in the spokes of a bicycle. Like a loose mainsail on a sailboat. Pandemonium. Chaos! Long, slimy stringers of snot flying in all directions, little round blobs of ectoplastic material flying about. Sort of like standing in a blizzard of wet slimy snow. Teenagers scattering every which way. One young woman cleaning goobers from her glasses, glaring myopically at me. Another with a truly impressive slime trail all the way down her leg. Hey, I tried to warn them. So much for popularity.

Becky (You DOLT! We were getting petted by a whole bunch of folks! You slimy knothead!)
Peggy Sue (Geez, Earnie, couldn't ya have done that somewhere else? Why couldn't you just fart, or something? Sheesh!)
Earnie (Whaddid I do? Why is everybody leaving? Hey, c'mon back—I looooovvvveeee you!)

Michael & Scotty Richardson
The Golden Gang
Becky: The Red Scourge of Squirrels, Feline Track Coach
Peggy Sue: Pixie, Lover of Every Creature, Fecal Gourmet
Earnie: Marriage Test, former Great White Humper
Living in SW Washington State, USA

ROPE A DOPE—KNOTHEAD?

My golden boy, Earnie (the airhead), has been something of a problem to find unbreakable toys for, as some of you are surely aware. He's systematically slaughtered every woobie in the house some the girls had for years. Then began the elimination of rubber toys, one by one. Holds 'em down with one foot and rips 'em to shreds. Then he eats the shreds. So far we've found two things he cannot immediately destroy: hard rubber "Kongs" and baseball-bat-sized cotton rope pulls. He does manage to ingest the cotton ropes over a period of time, but the biggest ones available last about six months before going the way of all that enters the pooper-scooper. Interesting, he poops string-wrapped parcels. All we'd need to do to ship them would be to address 'em. Wonder how the UPS guy would like that? Anybody out there want an Earniegram? I'll do the postage?

Earnie's method of "play" with these heavy rope pulls is interesting. If you haven't seen one of these, the rope is about three inches in diameter, about three feet long, and has a *big* knot on each end, the size of a large man's fist. These things are heavy! Earnie grabs the rope near the center and shakes his head violently from side to side, beating himself about the head and shoulders until he gets dizzy and falls to his knees. As soon as he comes around enough to regain what little coordination he generally possesses (he's about as agile as a cow on stilts), he does it some more!

Big horrid thuds and thumps as the knots bounce from his anatomy pain me to listen to. Sounds like a vicious heavyweight fight. Sure a good thing his head is empty; no chance of brain damage, I guess. This rope-a-dope game gets even nastier if he's played with the rope for a while, because he drools all over it so when he shakes it, snot and spittle fly all over the room. Even Becky and The Pigger just get up and leave when that starts. Must be another "guy" thing, eh? Ah ya gotta love 'em!

Becky (If he'd had any sense he's beating it out of himself, the idjut. Typical dumb blonde.)
Peggy Sue (Hey, this isn't a blonde thing! It's an airhead thing, and airheads come in all colors!)
Earnie (Thump! Thud! Oof! Geez, that hurts! Duhhhhh let's do that some more! Thudthumpclobberoof!)

Michael & Scotty Richardson
The Golden Gang
Becky: The Red Scourge of Squirrels, Feline Track Coach
Peggy Sue: Pixie, Lover of Every Creature, Fecal Gourmet
Earnie: Marriage Test, former Great White Humper
Living in SW Washington State, USA

SLIMY CROTCH SYSNDROME?

Thought I'd pass this on to see if there are others out there suffering from this malady. It was suggested I give Earnie street hockey balls to play with, as he wouldn't be able to destroy them. This is probably true.

One small problem with this—if Earnie has a ball, any kind of a ball, *he will drive me nuts with it!* He shoves it in my face, in my crotch, my lap, my armpit, etc., until I'm ready to explode! Naturally, the ball is thoroughly *slimed* before he presents it to me. This causes the crotch area of my Levis to have shiny, slick, lugubrious patches of dog snot (pupkus?) on them. I don't know why, but this makes strangers nervous. They place a protective arm about their children in the supermarket and sidle away from me, keeping a careful watch. Even grandmothers tend to move away from the freezer cases until I'm clear of it. People lose eye contact when they talk to me, they keep looking down suspiciously. I notice police cars in the parking lot with officers sorting through photographs and staring at me. I mean I like attention as well as the next person, but hey, what's going on here?

Becky (There used to be balls in the house to play with, and now you hide them from us!)

Peggy Sue (Balls, schmalz, who cares? Buffalo nose can slime you without the benefit of a ball!)

Earnie (Hey, anybody wanna play ball with me? Huh? Do ya? Why are you running away?)

Michael & Scotty Richardson
The Golden Gang

308

Becky: The Red Scourge of Squirrels, Feline Track Coach
Peggy Sue: Pixie, Lover of Every Creature, Fecal Gourmet
Earnie: Marriage Test, former Great White Humper
Living in SW Washington State, USA

HONEY, I ATE THE BEDS

Earnie, our fur-bearing shredder, has done it again! Add another chapter to his toy-totaling, woobie-wrecking, furniture fubar activities! Oh I'm sooooo proud! During his stay at Susie's Country Inn, a very fancy (and expensive) kennel here in town, he totally destroyed two dog beds. Now there were *three* dog beds in that run with Becky, Peggy Sue, and The Earnster. He only ate *two* of 'em. Which two? Why, the girls beds, of course! Perhaps Ol' Dimbulb ain't as dumb as we think, eh? Becky's bed was particularly shredded. Peggy Sue's was repairable. Hmmmm. Message to the Alpha Bitch? We first learned of his midnight activities during a long distance call from Utah to check on the "kids." Susie didn't sound too happy—she had to take all the beds away as Earnie was actually ingesting the foam rubber from one bed. Pooping nerf-balls. Dangerous. Also he was continuing his favorite kennel activity—fence-fighting. Bear in mind he had been neutered only two weeks prior to his kennel stay, so the hormones in his overactive system hadn't really cleared out yet. Susie's is where we took his obedience classes. He and Susie are on first-name terms. She said she "straightened him out on the fence-fighting." I didn't ask how. I don't want to know! I do know this lady is a heck of a good trainer and uses only *very* humane methods. I trust her. At any rate, he and the girls are now home and all seems to be well. We can see a big difference in his temperament since neutering. More mellow, hasn't humped a single piece of furniture this week! Peggy Sue no longer sleeps with her butt in the corner. Becky isn't so busy giving him attitude adjustments! My wife is sewing up the beds. Ah home sweet home!

Becky (I slept on a cold, hard cement floor because of that little varmint! I'll get even!)

Peggy Sue (Yeah, me too! Let's stuff him in the freezer for a night. See how he likes that!)

Earnie (You took away my manhood, you warehoused me, you didn't leave me anything to chew on—just 'cause I squabble with Becky over chewies—so I ate the beds! Hahahahah! But I only ate *two* of 'em! Get it? Kinda like the Donner Party judge said—"There was only ten Democrats in the whole county, and you et three of 'em!")

Michael & Scotty Richardson
The Golden Gang
Becky: The Red Scourge of Squirrels, Feline Track Coach
Peggy Sue: Pixie, Lover of Every Creature, Fecal Gourmet
Earnie: Marriage Test, Woobie Shredder, former Great White Humper
Living in SW Washington State, USA

THE BITCH HAS BALLS!

Becky did a pretty funny thing today. We've had the dogs kenneled the last few weeks while we were doing some wilderness canoeing. They didn't get their "normal" exercise routine, generally consisting of a daily four- to five-mile on-lead walk combined with chasing tennis balls off-lead in a large field below our home. Most days, I continue to swat balls as far as I can until Becky has had enough. She's always been the strongest of the dogs, possessing the most endurance. Today, it being a nice cool day and having dealt with Earnie's "busy times" (ARRRGGGHHHH!) the last couple of days, I decided to *show no mercy* while swatting balls. Last dog standing! Until today, that's always been Becky. I hit balls. The dogs chased them. They chased them some more. Peggy Sue had enough; she lied down in the field and watched the other two go at it. Earnie and Becky, head to head, foaming at the mouths. Until today, Earnie has always quit before Becky. Not today; Becky finally had enough, retrieved a ball and instead of returning to me, she took it across the field where she laid herself down next to it, lurking in the high grass. Earnie, in the meantime, continued to retrieve balls thinking, I'm sure, he was finally rid of the Red Bitch. Not for long! Becky waited until she had a clear shot at getting to a ball before Earnie, and out of the high grass, she charged, grabbed the ball, and took it back to her "lair" where she stashed the ball with her other one. OK, I had a whole sack of balls. Before long, Becky had them "all" in a pile lying next to her, far across the field. Earnie and The Pigger were looking at her with "please, Becky, can we have a ball?" looks. Becky's look said "just try for one, make my day!" Game over. Alpha Bitch wins. Red dog, 10; blondes, 0.

Peggy Sue (Ball hog! Just when I was getting my second wind too!)

Earnie (I finally outran ya, and your ego just couldn't take it, huh? Nyah! Nyah!)

Becky (These are *my* balls, this is *my* game, and I AM IN CHARGE HERE! We play fetch when *I* say we play fetch, dammit! Dumb blondes, anyhow.)

Michael & Scotty Richardson
The Golden Gang
Becky: The Red Scourge of Squirrels, Feline Track Coach
Peggy Sue: Pixie, Lover of Every Creature, Fecal Gourmet
Earnie; Marriage Test, Woobie Shredder, former Great White Humper
Living in SW Washington State, USA

THE THREE-HOUR,
TWO-HOUR MOVIE

About a year ago, when Earnie was just a little tyke, we discovered he has a bit of a quirk. He can't stand for us to watch a home movie unmolested.

We thought it would get better. We were wrong. It's not better, and he's bigger. Picture being harassed by a seventy-pound hornet, you'll have some idea.

The following is a fairly accurate description of watching a movie with The Earnster:

Insert disc into laser player, hit (play) motor winds up. So does dog.

Begin watching movie. Dog finds ball from somewhere, shoves slimy tennis ball under your legs while "marfing" tennis ball, inadvertently bites your leg as well as tennis ball. Owner yelps with pain, curses. (Pause) Catch dog. Remove slimy, goobered ball from sloppy dog's jowls. Hide ball on refrigerator. Towel dog snot off hands. (Play) Watch five minutes of show.

Dog finds large cotton knot from chew rope, thoroughly slimes it. Dog shoves rope which smells like a combination of dead earthworms and anal glands under your legs. Dog pushes hard with buffalo-sized nose. Manages to push rope knot into rather tender area of owner's crotch. Owner curses. (Pause) Owner hides rope knot on refrigerator, goes upstairs and returns with several nice chewies. Offers dog chewies. Dog accepts chewies. Dog appears placated, even happy! (Play) Ten minutes goes by without interruption. Dog gets bored with chewie, begins tossing it in air and batting it about, like a cat. Manages to drop chewie on sleeping alpha bitch. Alpha bitch is not pleased. Dog tries

314

to remove chewie from under alpha bitch. Alpha bitch shows teeth. Dog then circles alpha bitch, barking loudly. (Pause) Owner gets out of recliner, removes chewie from danger zone which surrounds alpha-bitch. Returns chewie to dog. (Play)

Owners watch twenty minutes of movie. Dog goes to patio door, rings bell. Dog needs out. (Pause) Dog goes out, doesn't want to come back in. It's raining, naturally. Owner finally gets dog in by yelling "cookies!" Dog is wet. Owner is wet. Dog is cheerful. Owner is not. (Play) Dog munches happily on chewie for ten minutes. Gets bored. Gets the FRAPs (frenetic rapid activity periods). Does a couple of flip turns off the futon, upon which Peggy Sue and my wife are seated. Neither is pleased. (Pause) Catch dog, now hyperventilating with wild look in eyes. Pet dog, speak in calming voice (difficult when you're fantasizing about how roast dog tastes at this point), get back in recliner, invite dog to sit in chair with you. Dog likes to be in recliner with owner. Dog gets in chair with you. (Play) Enjoy twenty to thirty minutes of movie. Dog is napping, snoring loudly. Turn up volume to cover snoring. Dang! Time to turn disc over. Owner has to move out of chair. Dog wakes up from nap, refreshed. Repeat the above during the second half of movie, until credits roll and the music plays. Movie over. Dog goes to sleep for the night.

Becky (If he whaps me with that chew bone *one* more time, he's *meat!*) Peggy Sue (It used to be safe sleeping on the futon. Now it's like napping on the freeway!) Earnie (Hey whatcha watching? I kinda liked *Homeward Bound.* I could identify with that dog, Chance was his name, I think. I almost watched that movie, but I guess I got kinda bored. Anybody wanna play ball? Hey what's with the dirty looks?)

Michael & Scotty Richardson
The Golden Gang
Becky: The Red Scourge of Squirrels, Feline Track Coach
Peggy Sue; Pixie, Lover of Every Creature, Fecal Gourmet
Earnie: Marriage Test, Woobie Shredder, former Great White Humper
Living in SW Washington State, USA

RUNNIN' STYLES

A thought occurred to me today (at my age, that in itself was a revelation) as I watched my three Furbuggers retrieving tennis balls. They are all goldens. In my eyes, of course, they're all *perfect and beautiful.*
But they are each *very* different. I decided to critique their running styles, blinders removed. Pure, unadulterated criticism. I figure hey, I can shake off the stardust long enough to be critical of my wife, so why not the dogs? As I watched each dog run, I made mental notes. See below for the results.

Dog no. 1. Becky. Fluid, graceful, powerful, energetic, nimble, a pure delight to observe! Picture a gazelle, an antelope, a cheetah. This dog has suffered nearly all of the paw/pad injuries we've had in this family because she also tends to be reckless, fearless, willing to sacrifice her body in order to *get that tennis ball!*

Dog no. 2. Peggy Sue. Conservative, barrel-chested, choppy runner. Capable of quick bursts of speed, unable to maintain them. Picture a white rhino sans horn, a sprinter's heavy build. Prefers rolling on tennis balls to retrieving them. Unwilling to make physical sacrifices to the tennis-ball gods. Hell with it. Let Becky get the stoopid ball. Would rather root around for disgusting stuff to eat or roll in than retrieve.

Dog no. 3. Earnie. Difficult to describe. Loose-jointed runner. Flaps around all over the place. Picture goosing a bag lady. Picture a cow on stilts. Capable of great speed, endurance unknown. Never been able to wear him out. Tends to lead with his head. Dives at tennis balls at top speed, generally misses them. Can pack four tennis balls at a time.

Loves to do double-retrieves, usually at Becky's expense. Really knows how to slime a tennis ball too.

Becky (Did you tell them how I can catch tennis balls that you hit way up in the air? Makes a sound like a catcher's mitt!)
Peggy Sue (What's the big deal about retrieving, anyway? Any idiot can do that. Just watch Becky. Eating *just the right poop*, now THERE'S an art!)
Earnie (Whaddayamean, flap around? Hey, I'm just sauntering when I do that! I think I can outrun Becky now!)

Michael & Scotty Richardson
The Golden Gang
Becky: The Red Scourge of Squirrels, Feline Track Coach
Peggy Sue: Pixie, Lover of Every Creature, Fecal Gourmet
Earnie: Marriage Test, Woobie Shredder, former Great White Humper
Living in SW Washington State, USA

TIRING EARNIE

I think we found a way to get some peace in the evenings! Earnie is fourteen months old now and a real dynamo. If you have followed any of my prior postings, you know how *nuts* he can make us when we try to watch a movie or do anything where he's not a required part of the action! Usually, writing on this computer is a contact sport. Large slobber-covered chin whumping the keyboard from time to time. Makes proper spelling difficult.

But tonight, he is sleeping, as are the other two! Peace and quiet! Ahhhh!

All it took was taking the three of them along on a mushroom field trip we led today. The area we hunted is incredible—*real* old growth fir trees, some probably thirty feet in diameter. A marvelously clear stream runs along the bottom of the canyon. The weather was *perfect* golden weather—forty degrees and raining hard! I pulled the truck off the road and kicked the dogs out. Off they went! They ran, they swam, they stomped on mushrooms we were trying to harvest. The stream is running very swift right now with all the rain. They fetched sticks swimming against the current; that really works them! Earnie wouldn't go into the creek last year—this year you couldn't keep him out of it! He's becoming a strong swimmer. He has also learned one of my least favorite dog tricks. He grabs a big limb and tries to run past you on the trail with it. I am not thrilled about that. The bruises on the back of my legs are why. Anyhow, the furkids were off lead and really rockin' and rollin' *all* day. Then home, three dog baths, dinner and sleep!

Gotta love 'em, eh? BTW, I see hunting mentioned in another post. The deer hunters are out in the area we were in today. I have bells on each dog, and use florescent surveyors ribbon tied liberally all about their collars to alert hunters that they're *not* game. So far, it's worked. The danger of a dog being shot is always there this time of the year. Unfortunately, mushrooms fruit during deer and elk seasons out here in Washington. I figure it's a calculated risk allowing my dogs to run free where there are hunters. I constantly cross my fingers, so far, after eight years, nobody's taken a shot at us or the dogs yet! Knock on wood!

Becky (Whew! I'm tired! That blonde brat is getting tougher to keep up with!)
Peggy Sue (I just bop along with the old folks. I don't even try to keep up with those two idjuts!)
Earnie (Hey, wow! The woods are my favorite place! Watch me dive into the creek, guys! Wheeeeee! Boy, am I ever tired!)

Michael & Scotty Richardson
The Golden Gang
Becky: The Red Scourge of Squirrels, Feline Track Coach
Peggy Sue: Pixie, Lover of Every Creature, Fecal Gourmet
Earnie: Marriage Test, Woobie Shredder, former Great White Humper
Living in SW Washington State, USA

EARNIE, FUNGAL GOURMET?

A fine day here in the NW. Today, we took the *furkids* up the Washougal River, into the headwater area for a mushroom hunt. What a day! Picture-perfect weather, sixty-five degrees, sunny, beautiful fall colors, pristine, perfectly clear water in the river. Salmon spawning in some of the gravel beds. We started our mushroom hunt in the lower elevations, around two thousand feet, looking primarily for chanterelles. Great fun! Remember as a child how you loved Easter egg hunts? Picture an Easter egg hunt for adults and you'll have an idea of the fun we have! Today, we had luck! Incredible luck! In forty-five minutes, we had over thirty pounds of beautiful specimens! Enough to use all winter. The dogs were having a total hoot running amok in the woods, doing inscrutable dog things, like eating deer poop. Peggy Sue and Becky usually eat chanterelles as we pick them, sometimes we have to fight the dogs for the 'shrooms! Today, as the 'shrooms were plentiful, we let them eat all they wanted. Earnie has decided he doesn't like chanterelles. He leaves 'em to the girls. After hauling the mushrooms back to the truck, we decided to go higher and search for *Boletus edulis,* one of my favorite edibles and usually a difficult mushroom to find. After twelve miles of bad roads, some of which required low range in my 4×4, we found ourselves at about four thousand feet. Lo and behold, after a short hike of perhaps a mile, we encountered dozens of huge boletes! I was happily kneeling and picking when I heard a huge, wet *belch* right behind me. Earnie was eating all the trimmings I was leaving from the boletes! Interesting, as the girls won't eat boletes.

Must be another "guy" thing? Earnie is turning into quite the little woodsman; he isn't into chasing deer like Becky. He's always within one hundred feet or so of us as we crash through the brush. It's really a great pleasure to see the fun the dogs have out in the woods! It's also a great pleasure having an evening of peace and quiet while they sleep off their trip! (VBG)

Becky (I didn't chase a single deer today! Good thing too. Hunting season is open! Could get shot!)
Peggy Sue (I ate sooooo many chanterelles! Yummy!)
Earnie (Boletes are my favorites! They taste a little like roasted hazelnuts! Mmmmm good! BELCH!)

Michael & Scotty Richardson
The Golden Gang
Becky: The Red Scourge of Squirrels, Feline Track Coach
Peggy Sue: Pixie, Lover of Every Creature, Fecal Gourmet
Earnie: Marriage Test, Woobie Shredder, Former Great White Humper
Living in SW Washington State, USA

THE HOT TUB TERRORIST?

Earnie, aka PITA (pronounced "pete-ah," as in "pain in the ass") has found a new way to annoy me. Amazing! I thought he'd found all possible means of irritating us. Eating the futon and other selected furniture items. Getting the evening FRAPs, causing much damage to the carpets. Digging up, and eating my wife's flowers. Farting while lying in the recliner with me. Loudly, I might add. All the normal stuff. Add one to the list! The other day, my friend arrived at our house looking stressed, so I suggested a nice soak in the hot tub. My offer was accepted, so in the tub we went. Normally, Becky, our no. 1 dog lies at the top of the steps to the hot tub if we're in it, waiting patiently for us to get out, happy if she gets an occasional head-pat. Peggy Sue firmly believes the hot tub is terribly evil and that it's out to get her, hence she avoids it. Earnie, until last weekend, has also ignored the hot tub if we're soaking and gone about his merry way causing major lawn damage while we aren't watching his every move. After we'd been in the tub for a few minutes, Earnie decided to climb the steps to say "howdy." Unfortunately, he had a very slimy, large dirty ball he'd scrounged from somewhere in his mouth. He gave a big Earnie-smile with his tail wagging madly and dropped said filthy ball in the hot tub. Probably because he's not coordinated enough to wag and smile at the same time. This is where my friend made *the fatal error* of automatically throwing the ball out into the yard for Earnie. Arrggghhh!

Understand, my friend is used to Becky and Peggy Sue who will *go away* if you suggest it to them. They know when you aren't interested in play. They have brains! Earnie's brain, if it exists (questionable) must be about the size of a pea. Picture a marble in a fish bowl. Telling Earnie to *go away* or *knock it off* has exactly the same effect it would if used on a swarm of blackflies. Like yelling at a yellow jacket, mosquitoes, or horseflies.

It just turns him on. So back he comes, again and again and again and again with the ball, each time obviously going to some effort to roll it in something really disgusting before delivering it to us. The usual reason one soaks in a hot tub is to relax. Relaxing is difficult with a seventy-pound hound dribbling a dirty ball down your neck every thirty seconds or so. The hot tub by now was full of unidentifiable, disgusting detritus. My friend decided to *hide* the ball. Ha! Earnie figured that out in about a heartbeat. Earnie bunched his muscles and prepared to launch himself into the hot tub to get *the ball*; so we opted to just throw the damned thing. A dirty ball in the tub is one thing, Earnie is another. Ah you gotta love 'em!

Becky (Not only was he dropping that ball in the hot tub, he was climbing over me to do it! Grrrrrr.)
Peggy Sue (I dunno why anyone would get near that thing! It makes funny sucking noises! One day, it's coming, I just know it is!)
Earnie (Oboy! A new game! Dontcha just LOVE to play ball with me, hey dad, huh dad, hey, hey, hey, isn't this just great fun! Why are you getting out already? Huh? Doesn't it feel good? Here, here's the ball!)

Michael & Scotty Richardson
The Golden Gang
Becky: The Red Scourge of Squirrels, Feline Track Coach
Peggy Sue: Pixie, Lover of Every Creature, Fecal Gourmet
Earnie: Marriage Test, Woobie Shredder, General PITA
Living in SW Washington State, USA

END OF VOLUME ONE

I have never written any type of book. Surely, to anyone who has ever read a book, that is painfully obvious. But I am told that around sixty-five thousand words is an average book. Of course, this is NOT an average book. It's a bit different and, I hope, entertaining to most who take their valuable time to read it. If it brought a few chuckles, that's what I hope for. Now notice if you will, Earnie is still a pup. There is *much* to come, as these particular snippets ended in 1997. If there is any profit from this book, half of it or more will be donated to Golden Retriever Rescue. Bless you people who take your time and money to rescue dogs who are abused or just not wanted. So hey, if you like it, I will carry on to volume two sometime soon. There is some really funny stuff in there! But then, these dogs are a laugh a minute if you look at them that way!

Scotty Richardson
March 2015